As the parent of a teen, are you ready to accept these undeniable truths?

Axioms: *Eleven to Thirteen* A teenager's definition of deprivation is a house with one phone, one car, one TV, and no junk food.

A twelve-year-old girl will have at least three "best friends" in a given week.

Axioms: *Fourteen to Seventeen* Most families stop going out for dinner as soon as their children develop a taste for lobster.

A boy capable of rebuilding a carburetor is not necessarily capable of making his bed.

Axioms: *Eighteen to Twenty-one* If college is less than three hours from home, Laundromats are optional.

Your child's roommate is telling his parents the same horror stories about your son that you're hearing about him.

The delightful pages of *Lord, Don't You Get Frustrated With Teens Too?* will help you discover the funny side of parenting teens.

"Lord, Don't You Get Frustrated with Teenagers Too?"

BY Toni Sortor

From Training Pants to
Training Wheels

Lord, Don't You Get Frustrated
With Teenagers Too?

"Lord, Don't You Get Frustrated with Teenagers Too?"

TONI SORTOR

Power Books

Fleming H. Revell Company
Old Tappan, New Jersey

All Scripture quotations in this book are taken from the King James Version of the Bible.

Library of Congress Cataloging-in-Publication Data

Sortor, Toni, 1939–
    Lord, don't you get frustrated with teenagers too? / Toni Sortor.
      p. cm.
    "Power books."
    ISBN 0-8007-5319-4
    1. Teenagers—Prayer-books and devotions—English. I. Title.
BV4850.S65 1989
248.8'45—dc20   89-33412
                                              CIP

For Bill

Contents

Introduction

Does the world really need another book on raising teenagers? Probably not—there are certainly plenty of them out there, written by people with more credentials than I'll ever have or want.

But if you like to laugh at yourself now and then . . . if you love your kids, no matter what horrible stage they're going through . . . if you wish you could find a Scripture verse to get you through a particularly dreadful day, or a prayer that expresses what you're feeling . . . maybe what you need is another mother to talk to, not another expert.

Lots of us have been where you are now and survived to tell about it. We're the ones in the supermarket checkout line, whimpering while we write checks for $150 on accounts with balances of $155 (*if* that last deposit finally cleared). We drive old station wagons with dinged fenders that should have little signs on them proclaiming, "*I* didn't do it!" We smile a lot at other people's babies, remembering the good old days and trying not to say, "Just wait until. . . "

I have three children in various stages of young adulthood: a daughter of twenty-four, a son of twenty-one, and another son of seventeen. I'm beginning to see the light at the end of the tunnel, you might say. If I can survive it, so can you. Maybe this will help a little.

"Lord, Don't You Get Frustrated with Teenagers Too?"

1 Definitions

You can take the word *teenager* literally, if you want: The years between thirteen and twenty apply then. Or you can be more realistic and face the fact that a girl may become a teenager as early as eleven or twelve, while a boy usually stays a boy until fourteen or fifteen. At the other end, the teenage years come to a close when the kids graduate from college or move out; although we all know some thirty-five-year-old teenagers, don't we? For our purposes, we'll consider anyone a teenager as soon as his hormones start pushing him around and consider him an adult whenever he starts supporting himself.

It's not as simple to define a *parent* as it used to be. We now have step-parents and biological parents, full-time parents and weekend parents, single parents and combined-family parents. They all carry some of the load. Generally, we're talking about whatever adults accept the day-to-day responsibility, though: the ones who will be called to bail out any given teenager at 2:00 A.M.

Home is easier to define: It's where, when a teenager

shows up at the door, they have to let him in. It's where he keeps his stereo. Most of the time, it's where his parents, as defined above, live, although sometimes you can't even count on that. I remember my sense of shock and outrage when my college son spoke of college as his "home." I told him *this* was his home; college was just where he lived nine months of the year. But I knew in my heart he was right and I was wrong. I just didn't want to admit it yet.

Life used to be simpler, didn't it? That's one of the difficulties of parenting a teenager: Suddenly nothing is simple anymore. When your children were young, you had all the answers. You were all-powerful in their lives, and they respected that. They did what you told them to do because you were self-confident and they believed in you—and you were considerably bigger than they were.

None of which applies anymore. The world has changed so drastically since you were a teenager that you no longer have all the answers. Some days you're not even sure you understand the questions! And your children, although deep down they still believe in you as a person, are no longer willing to take your word for anything. What's more, they're now considerably bigger and stronger than you are, which tells you something about the potency of today's vitamins and junk food.

Parents don't take all this very well. They get moody and pout or they lose it and yell, neither of which helps a lot. There's a long, crooked, foggy, potholed road to travel between twelve and twenty, but somehow most families do get there in one piece. The lucky ones arrive to find their teenagers have turned into their friends along the way. That's nice.

Father, I'm a little afraid of being a teenager's parent. You know what's out there these days. I don't have any experience in a lot of the things my children will have to make decisions about. All I can do is try my best and ask You to guide us through the years to come.

So foolish was I, and ignorant: I was as a beast before thee. Nevertheless I am continually with thee: thou hast holden me by my right hand. Thou shalt guide me with thy counsel. . . .

Psalms 73:22–24

2

Axioms:
Eleven to Thirteen

Brothers who spit peas at each other at home must be carefully watched in restaurants.

A twelve-year-old girl will have at least three "best friends" in a given week.

All notes from you to a teacher will be lost on the way to school; all notes from a teacher to you will decompose in the bottom of a schoolbag.

Volunteer work has driven more mothers into full-time work than the need for a second income.

No parent should be allowed within shouting distance of a Little League game.

If a child can see over the ticket counter, he can buy his way into an R-rated movie.

A child who says he has no homework is lying.

Puppy love hurts as much as the real thing when it's over.

If you have only one son to mow the lawn, he'll develop hay fever as soon as he's old enough to be trusted with the lawn mower.

A teenager's definition of deprivation is a house with one phone, one car, one TV, and no junk food.

3   Eleven

Yes, eleven. My sweet, cooperative ten-year-old daughter had just turned eleven. I had almost recovered from toilet training child number three and number one was only eleven. Heaven! I had at least two years to recuperate before my first foray into the teens. *Good timing*, I congratulated myself. *You deserve a little rest.* Then she turned around and bit my head off.

It was unexpected, but it was soon over; in ten minutes, she was back to being her normal cheerful self. We floated along for a few days—good buddies shopping together, taking care of the two boys, deciding what we wanted to cook for dinner. Then I mentioned her hair was getting a little scraggly. When did she want me to make the appointment? She burst into tears, ran up to her room, and locked herself in until her father came home.

After a few weeks of living on this emotional roller coaster, I dug out Dr. Spock, who promptly informed me that my daughter's behavior was perfectly normal—for a girl entering puberty. Puberty? The kid was a great softball player—who was ready for hormones? Who *needs* them, at eleven?

Apparently she did.

If you've never lived with a girl this age, just recall everything you've ever read about menopause and imagine it happening to an immature, unprepared eleven-year-old. It's basically the same process in reverse, and the emotional fallout's the same: mood swings, paranoia, nonexistent self-esteem, lack of stability. It's bad enough facing menopause yourself in a few years, without your daughter giving you a preview of coming detractions.

Well, there's no way around it now. Might as well resign yourself to a very interesting year. Just don't expect to do anything right for a while. If you tell her she needs a bra, she'll run off and lock herself in her room. Tell her she doesn't need one, she'll run off. . . . You get the idea.

It would be okay if it were logical—if you could keep the

peace by simply not mentioning anything about her body, her clothes, and her hair, for example. It's not that simple. You'll see that pimple sprouting on her forehead and wisely decide not to mention it—not even to *look* at it. Then her father will breeze in, do a double take, and tell her, "Hey, you've got a big goober on your forehead!" You'll brace yourself for the sound of slamming doors, only to hear her laugh in reply. Ten minutes later you'll lovingly brush her hair out of her eyes and she'll go off like a firecracker. You never know from day to day what's acceptable and what's dangerous.

Other times, she couldn't be more loving, more tender with her baby brother, more concerned about those migraine headaches you're developing.

You want to gather her up on your lap and tell her it's okay, that you remember what she's going through and it'll pass, that you think she's wonderful and you'll always love her. But she won't let you. You have to sneak it in when you can and hope the message gets through.

Hang on. It will pass. Soon the first rush of hormones will even out and she'll learn how to handle them. But do go see the doctor about those migraines. It's probably the only time in your life he'll be right when he says it's hormones!

This is a confusing time for both of us, Lord. One minute she's playing with her beloved dolls, the next she's campaigning to wear makeup. I'm not quite ready to lose the little girl I've come to enjoy so much, but I am looking forward to the woman she's becoming. Help us keep our cool until we're past this rough spot.

A soft answer turneth away wrath: but grievous words stir up anger.

Proverbs 15:1

4

Games

Games have changed since I was a teenager. Since we didn't have TV or air-conditioning or stereo, and did have limited spending money, I grew up playing a lot of games. None of which my children would ever think of playing. We played board games in bad weather, word games on car rides, pitch-and-catch, hide-and-seek, and long, involved war games on sunny days. Some kids, the ones you were never too sure of, even pitched pennies against the school's walls before the doors opened in the mornings. Games were what children did when no adults were around telling them to go mow the lawn.

If they get really desperate—after being snowed in for three days during a power failure, for example—we might all agree on a game of Monopoly, but that's very rare. It's also very dangerous, since two out of the five of us are very sore losers and it takes a whole day of cajoling to get them speaking to the winners. I won't name names here, but the soreheads are both males. Luckily, they usually win.

Once a year I'll dump a thousand-piece jigsaw puzzle out on the dining room table and we'll all get sore backs from working on it. No one is so jaded that he can resist a puzzle, even if he only works on it on the sly.

We tried Trivial Pursuit. No one will play with me anymore, and I'm not about to have another child in hopes of conning him into a game or two. Some wiseguy teenager would probably warn him not to play with Mommy before he got out of his high chair.

The only games they really enjoy playing are ones that play back. One little handheld electronic football game has seen them through hours of backseat deprivation; *deprivation* being defined as not having an outlet available for plugging in a game. There's nothing worse than driving two hundred miles in one day with a teenager, unless it's driving two hundred miles and being forced to listen to one of those games bleeping away in the backseat.

At home, they started out with an Atari that plugged into the TV, then progressed to playing games on their father's computer. (You want to talk about games? What about men and their computers?) In desperation, Bill finally broke down and bought them their own little computer, which has never done any computing but has lived a productive life as a game player.

I play computer games, too, so I can't really complain. They're wonderful on rainy weekends when you just can't stand to do another load of laundry. Except that my kids play them so much *better* than I do! I try to fly an aircraft simulator and find I can't get out of the hangar. I play a war game and tanks run right over me. I take on one of those all-word, role-playing games, and the computer tells me it doesn't understand what I mean when I tell it I want to "Run away!" In five minutes, I'm yelling at the stupid machine and my sons are rolling on the floor in hysterics.

They also play a new type of board game with a million tiny cardboard markers and a rulebook that's at least a hundred pages long. I recognize tanks on some of the pieces, so it's obviously a war game. It also takes up the whole kitchen table and goes on for days once it's set up. This is not something I can comprehend, like Sorry! or checkers.

As much as I get annoyed by the bleeps, buzzes, and splats that come from the computer games and the tiny tank pieces dropped on the floor during their board games, I do have to admit one thing: These kids are playing very difficult, complex games that I never could have mastered at their age. These games take more patience than chess ever did, more dexterity of hand and brain than Parcheesi or Uno or anything I ever played. Their games, without a doubt, are simply better than ours, and that makes me rather jealous.

Now if you'll excuse me, I'm going to go play the computer a game of Scrabble. By the way, the computer cheats! I like that; it makes it seem as if I'm playing a real person. Besides, my son just showed me how to cheat back!

Even though forms of play change through the years, playing remains an important part of life, a part designed and approved by You, Father. Let me allow them to enjoy their play while they can.

. . . Provide me now a man that can play well. . . .

1 Samuel 16:17

5

Chores

Chores and allowances should not be related to each other, but on the day before allowances are paid, they usually are. Theoretically, chores are assigned and completed simply because the child is a functioning member of the family, expected to pull his weight. Financial considerations should have nothing whatsoever to do with the performance of chores. Allowances are freely given as spending money, lunch money, or money to be saved for future needs. They shouldn't relate to chores.

So much for theory.

No one lives up to that ideal; many parents don't even bother to explain it to their kids. I thought it was an important (if moot) point and would run through it every year when we renegotiated allowances—which was the wrong time, if I wanted to be consistent, but just happened to be when I thought of it. It didn't matter; I never fooled a single kid with it.

Both sides are at fault in this. Children don't do their chores unless forced to, and parents withhold allowances to force children to do their chores. It's natural, on both sides, but it does undermine a vital point: Kids should be expected to contribute to the family's welfare.

Maybe it was easier in the old days, when children could easily see the value of their chores. The chickens obviously had to be fed, if anyone wanted Sunday dinner. Water had to be pumped or carried, or everyone would go thirsty and dirty. If the firewood wasn't chopped and carried, it would be a very cold evening for every member of the family.

It's not as obvious today. The garbage does have to be taken out, but there's no immediate danger of plague if it sits there and stinks until morning. Grass needs cutting every week during the summer, but one more day's growth isn't going to kill anyone. Civilization has taken much of the urgency out of childhood chores.

But the point behind chores is still valid. Children have to be taught that you sometimes do things altruistically— without thought of personal gain. You help those you love; you try to make things easier and better for them. A child takes out the garbage to help keep his home pleasant and relieve his overworked mother of a job he is capable of performing. He mows the lawn to help his overworked father and keep his home looking nice. He's contributing to the family's welfare, not to his own wallet.

I don't know if I ever successfully communicated that point to my children. They certainly don't go out of their way to look for new and exciting chores! But if I'm running low on milk, my daughter may remember to stop on her way home and buy some. My younger son will stop what he's doing and let the dog out if I'm busy. My older son takes his brother out to McDonald's for an unexpected treat now and then without being asked. Maybe they did catch on.

If so, I can't take much credit for it, because although I explained family responsibility to them often, I more often withheld their allowances until their chores were done! So much for theory.

It's such a long process, training a child in the important things of life, Lord. It's not like teaching him to drive, where he catches on and it's over. Important things take years to learn. Don't let me get so bogged down in the short lessons that I neglect the long-term ones, or, worse yet, totally forget to teach them.

And all thy children shall be taught of the Lord; and great shall be the peace of thy children.

Isaiah 54:13

6

Twelve

Twelve's not all that hard. Twelve-year-old boys know very well that the girls in their class are interested in them, but they feel no compulsion to return the interest. Like Ferdinand, they're content to sit out under a tree looking at the flowers blooming so profusely around them. The thought of actually touching a flower still makes them cringe, however.

They certainly aren't about to start taking unnecessary showers or get their hair styled. Bicycles, sports, and friends of their own sex still take up most of their time and energy. Parents are well-advised to leave things alone and let them go blithely on their way.

Girls of twelve have most likely gotten over the weepies and settled down to developing teenage interests, such as boys. This is the time for crushes on handsome teachers, fathers, and "older men" of thirteen or fourteen. These crushes involve a lot of giggling and some amateurish attempts at flirtation (done safely from within a group of other twelve-year-old girls), but not much else. Although they're devastated when their affection is not returned, nothing proves more embarrassing than actually having the object of their crush notice them. That provokes a panicky retreat and total reevaluation of the situation.

It's a rather silly year, but cute to watch, if you can stand the noise. You see, twelve-year-old girls are rarely alone. They're permanently attached to a collection of other girls, although the composition of the group will vary from week to week as one girl is dropped for some offense and another accepted on a trial basis.

Fortunately, the group needs privacy and meets in your daughter's room behind a locked door to prevent you or her brothers from interfering. About all you are required to do is keep the kitchen stocked and provide a telephone extension in her room.

Twelve was the year we put in what the phone company calls a teenager's line. This type of line has its own unlisted number, and the bill does come to you, but it also unties your phone line and saves you from having to yell "Get off the phone!" fifteen times a day. It's also pretty cheap, once you give her a list of towns in your local calling area and forbid her any other exchanges. Most importantly, you don't have to answer it if she's not home. Your parents didn't send you to college to answer a child's telephone calls and take messages from her giggling, breathless friends—most of whom have a crush on your husband and are calling in hopes of hearing his voice, not yours.

Despite all the changes taking place in her, a twelve-year-old girl is sometimes still a girl. She still plays sports, sometimes with the old crowd of boys she grew up playing with. Because she's begun to grow and they haven't, boys will either welcome her into their games so they can win or reject her because she's too good for them. It depends on how badly they want to win the game, in other words. Somehow a girl this age will manage to avoid any romantic notions about the boys she plays with; she can be "just friends" with the same boy her best friend adores. But then, it is hard to idolize a boy you can flatten anytime you want in a game of football.

Twelve is a little respite, a calm before the storm. Take advantage of it to build bridges between your child and yourself, because the dynamite years are on their way.

I'm sort of enjoying this year, Lord. She's having so much fun discovering and testing herself. She may not be sure who she is yet, but I think she's going to turn into a nice person when she's done. Give her Your guidance those times she can't ask for mine, and let her know it's going to work out okay.

That our sons may be as plants grown up in their youth; that our daughters may be as corner stones, polished after the similitude of a palace.

Psalms 144:12

7   Grand Union

J ust to show you how old I am, I once fed myself and my husband very well on $25 a week. Now I spend about that for a week's supply of Coke and milk.

The bill went up to $35 when we added formula and baby food to the list. Am I the only mother in the world who *never* succeeded in buying baby food without breaking at least one jar? Slippery little buggers. The stockboy would see me coming in the door and meet me at the baby-food aisle with his broom and mop. If by chance he missed me, the public-address system would soon proclaim, "Cleanup to the baby-food aisle." Even if I still needed more baby food, I'd be into the next aisle before the message was finished. Now I spend $35 a week in the frozen-food section alone.

As soon as they all got on human food, the bill escalated to $50. Luckily, hot dogs and hamburgers were their favorite foods for several wonderful years. If I don't buy steak, I can just barely get through the meat section for $50 now.

In case you're watching my math, I'm now up to $110, and I haven't bought pet food, paper products, or cleaning supplies yet. Not to mention the dairy aisle. With three full-grown teenagers in the house, I consider myself lucky to get out the door for $150.

As long as I could escape for $100 or so, I paid cash for

my food. Cash and coupons. But once it consistently edged over $100, I got nervous and applied for a Courtesy Card. The thought of publicly having to decide between toilet paper and dog food at the checkout counter was too much to bear. Why do they call it a Courtesy Card? Are they being courteous by taking my check, or am I supposed to be courteous enough to keep the check from bouncing? Do they expect anyone to be courteous when the register's mechanical voice yells out, "Total, one hundred sixty-three dollars and thirty-eight cents" and everyone in my line goes "Ohh," as though I'd just delivered a nine-pound baby?

I keep looking for my name on the cash register. You know, that little, not-so-subtle list that tells the cashier: DO NOT ACCEPT CHECKS FROM MRS. SORTOR. So far, so good.

Then there's the excruciating decision about which checkout line to pick. I usually try to find one that has a little baby at the end who's driving his mother crazy by throwing the *National Enquirer* to the floor. It's going to be a long, boring wait while my vegetables defrost, so I might as well have a baby to flirt with while I wait. I've never legally used an express line, although I once got talking to a neighbor I hadn't seen in a while and followed her into one. The mutterings behind me didn't soak in until it was too late, but the cashier was gracious about it and rang me up anyway.

I go through all this on my once-weekly shopping trip. This does not include trips to the deli for midweek cold cuts, to the produce stand for lettuce and corn, or back to the store for the kitty litter I didn't have room for in the cart. I don't actually know what I spend each week when it's all added up. It's probably more than I bring home in a week, however, and we don't eat that high on the hog. One way or another, we pay for it, but I wonder how others less fortunate than us do. It worries me.

Father, putting food on the table is such a basic responsibility, and it's getting harder every year. Thank You for providing us with enough to meet our needs; remind us of our obligation to help those who are having difficulty.

If a brother or sister be naked, and destitute of daily food, And one of you say unto them, Depart in peace, be ye warmed and filled; notwithstanding ye give them not those things which are needful to the body; what doth it profit?

James 2:15, 16

8

Redecorating

Once all your children become teenagers, you can do some selective redecorating. Not a total house job—that has to wait until the last child goes off to college—but enough to give you some hope and get rid of the institutional look you've been forced to live with.

For instance, if it's been at least six months since the last can of Coke was spilled, that brown rug in the family room can go. I know, you never bought a brown rug in your life, but an unbiased observer would never be able to tell that rug was originally gold. After all, it's been brown for fifteen years. You can probably try gold again with some success, but you're not ready for white yet.

If you're like me, you probably have armor-plated wallpaper in the kitchen. I started out with white washable paint until I discovered SpaghettiOs sauce never washes off. We sandblasted it and put on wallpaper that was about a quarter-inch thick and so glossy it served as a night-light. None of us, family or anyone in the immediate neighborhood, ever liked that paper, but it lasted for ten grungy years. I could take an SOS pad to it after a Jello-O fight and not even dim its luster. This year I took it down (it put up quite a fight) and repapered with a country print we all like. So far it's suffered from no outbreaks of rowdiness.

I made a mistake in the upstairs hall, though. That

paper wasn't of the same caliber as the kitchen paper, and fifteen years of scrubbing off handprints had left areas absolutely devoid of design. It had to go, but we weren't ready for the lovely eggshell white paint that replaced it. Well, I was ready; the kids weren't. Apparently their sense of balance isn't as developed as I thought and they still need to hang on to the walls as they go to their rooms.

The family room floor by the back door has been through several rebirths. It started out as lovely wide pine boards protected with paste wax. After a few years the boards had begun to buckle from the tracked-in rain and snow. We sanded it all down, refinished it, then put on six coats of poly. That would fix if forever, right? They've already worn through five and one-half coats of the poly, and I don't know what to try next.

We've owned three sets of sofas in twenty years. The ones we have now are beyond cleaning, but I'm not buying another one until all the pets go to their reward. If there's such a thing as cat heaven, I know it has plush sofas for shedding on and hiding mouse trophies. If we have overnight company, I always make my husband or one of the boys open up the sleeper sofa for me; they don't scream as loud as I do at whatever's hidden in there.

I solved the bathroom decorating problem years ago: Tile everything in sight and hose it down once a week. It looks a bit like a locker room, but they're still not ready for a designer bath.

We made one seemingly unwise purchase that turned out to be serendipitous. We took out the old gold (brown) wall-to-wall carpet in the living room/dining room and replaced it with two nice patterned area rugs. With a houseful of kids and pets, we were prepared to defend those rugs with our lives, but it wasn't necessary. The rugs don't even show dog hair, let alone Frito crumbs. And as we left our older son behind one weekend, we begged, "No party, please."

He replied, "With those rugs in the house? You think I'm crazy?" Guess they were a better investment than we thought!

I'm never going to own the house of my dreams. At least I hope I'm not. I can't think of anything more boring than a designer house with no children or pets running around.

Father, I like nice things as much as the next person, but not if owning them means a two-year-old can't stand on my sofa to see the snow falling outside. As I get older and crankier, help me remember that a home is for living in, not for looking at.

Lay not up for yourselves treasures upon earth, where moth and rust doth corrupt, and where thieves break through and steal: But lay up for yourselves treasures in heaven. . . . For where your treasure is, there will your heart be also.

Matthew 6:19–21

9
A Matter of Style

I admire parents who have their acts together, families where Mom and Dad always agree on discipline and both make use of the same style. They must produce very rational, secure children.

On the other hand, there's something to be said for keeping teenagers slightly off balance and wondering when the next bomb's going to drop. It gives you a slight advantage. With teens, you need every advantage you can scrape up.

I know parents who wouldn't think of punishing a teen before holding a conference and deciding on a mutually agreeable fate for their offspring. As far as I'm concerned, the parent who witnesses the offense has dibs and fires the first shot. Then, when the second parent gets home, he gets to mop up. I say this because I'm obviously a shoot-from-the-hip parent. That's my style.

Bill seems more rational, and generally is. Each child has gotten him really angry just once, and all three will go to any lengths to avoid witnessing that again; so a raised eyebrow or puckered mouth from him produces instant compliance. He can afford to reason with them. He can sleep on an offense and produce a sound, logical punishment the following morning. That's his style.

Our styles don't match. That doesn't mean we fight about it, though. First of all, if I'm mad enough to proclaim an unreasonable punishment ("Go to your room and don't come out until you're twenty-one!"), Bill's smart enough to go away until I calm down. In a little while I'll begin to feel foolish and he'll take over. That way we both get in our shots with no fighting between us.

It works out pretty well. In effect, we're playing "good cop, bad cop" with them. I'm the bad cop, naturally. When I'm done yelling, screaming, and swatting, he comes in and plays good cop. By then, they're so grateful to see a sane parent that they'll confess to anything just to keep me out of the room.

We aren't playing games with our kids, even though it sounds that way; we're just using our natural styles to good advantage. I'm sure there are families with "good cop" mothers, too. A family of two "bad cops" is probably loud but effective. Two "good cop" parents must be a teen's idea of heaven! Whatever works for you is fine by me; we all have our own styles.

Father, I'm not particularly happy being the bad guy, but that's my style. I know the kids manage to love me anyway. Thank You for giving me a good guy husband to balance things out and make it a little easier for us all.

. . . love covereth all sins.

Proverbs 10:12

10   The Big One-Three

Eighth grade. In our town, where elementary school goes through eighth grade, a thirteen-year-old boy is the top of the heap. They take control of the one basketball court during lunch hour and after school, muscling out any of the "little kids" who want to take a few shots. Their pushing and shoving take on new intensity as they slam dunk for the benefit of the girls watching from the sidelines. Ferdinand the Bull is beginning to feel his oats.

As well he might. At thirteen, my boys were taller than me and gaining fast on their father. (This is no big deal. We're a short family, still hoping to produce a child in the six-foot range. No luck so far.) They had shoulders and no hips and lots of feet. Their Adam's apples popped out, and their voices fell. Neither of them could beat their father at Indian wrestling yet, but the fight was harder, and Dad knew his time of physical supremacy was limited.

Neither of the boys had girlfriends at this age; who is it that's devastating all the thirteen-year-old girls? Seems to me there must be a few thirteen-year-old boys who develop early and sweep the field. You parents of thirteen-year-old girls better hope that's the case, because the alternative is a fifteen-year-old boy who's in high school and owns a moped!

The other possibility is that I simply didn't know about my sons' girlfriends at this age. There was a lot I didn't know about them—like where they were and what they were doing and if it was legal.

It's harder to keep track of a thirteen-year-old boy than of a girl the same age. For one thing, girls don't like to walk very far, so you at least know where they began the evening, because you dropped them off there. A boy will just tell you where he's starting from and walk off. Where they all go from there is anyone's guess. You can ask when they get home, but all you'll get is "around."

This isn't too much of a problem in our suburban area, because it's a long walk to anything that appeals to a thirteen-year-old. Most of the time they end up hanging around downtown or at a friend's house. Not that they can't get in plenty of trouble there or on the long walk home, but I didn't feel too nervous about it as long as their curfew was earlier than my bedtime. I made sure they all had quarters for their one phone call from police head-quarters and hoped for the best.

You do have some leverage with children this age: You can drive. Without your goodwill, they're cut off from the skating rink, the movies, even the eighth-grade graduation dance. The obverse of this is obvious: You are expected to be home by the phone in case your child needs a ride.

If you have a thirteen-year-old, you will spend a lot of surreptitious time on the telephone with other mothers of thirteen-year-olds. You'll sneak up to your room to call parents whose children are having parties. Will they be home? What time will the party be over? Are boys (girls) invited? What time should you pick up? At least once every six months, you will have to call around and do a curfew survey, because "everyone" stays out later than your child. Just pick the parents of the child you think is the sanest of the crowd and call them. You'll know who to call. If you have a son, another round of calls will be needed as soon as he starts crying poverty. The important thing is to make these calls now, while neither you nor your child will lose face. As they grow older, it's harder to admit you don't know what you're doing, but no parent of a thirteen-year-old knows anything with certainty, so there's no stigma attached to asking stupid questions.

You begin to worry about new things when your child hits thirteen. It's a worry you're not at all prepared for, either. Before, you worried about broken bones, bad grades, chipped teeth, and simple survival. All of those, you could more or less control through training and supervision. But that's past you, now. You are no longer physically with your child most of the day; he's off with a bunch of equally eager thirteen-year-olds, and most of the time, you won't know what's going on. This worry eats at you. It doesn't go away for years, but you do learn to come to some sort of agreement with it as time goes by. Maybe you just get numb.

Lord, I'm hanging onto the reins here, but someone's trying to pull away from me. It's too early to let go, isn't it? Help us both understand this, Lord. Give me a gentle hand on the reins; teach him not to fight the bit so much.

My son, if thine heart be wise, my heart shall rejoice, even mine. Yea, my reins shall rejoice, when thy lips speak right things.

Proverbs 23:15, 16

11 Family Vacations

No teenager wants to go on a family vacation unless it's expensive and guarantees an out-of-season suntan.

It's easy to meet the first requirement, since by the time they reach this age, you'll have to invest in two motel rooms every night and eat at least once a day in a restaurant. That in itself makes a car tour of Delaware expensive.

But who takes car trips with teenagers? We tried, but the only way any of us could stand it was when we owned a van and each child had his own private seat. They slept along the whole Blue Ridge drive, totally unconscious until we passed an electronic arcade at fifty-five miles an hour.

Arcades send out secret signals only teens can hear. On a once-in-a-lifetime family trip to England, we spent one week out of our three in arcades. Arcades on the seashore you expect, but an arcade next door to a fourteenth-century cathedral blows your mind.

If you habitually go to a little cabin on a secluded lake, you're in big trouble when your kids hit their teens. All the things they loved as children—fishing, boating, sunbathing, feeding chipmunks—are now *boring*. It got to the point where we had to let each child bring along a friend on these vacations, which meant we housed and fed six teens in a one-room log cabin. It was no vacation, and we were no family!

Teens always beg to be left at home as vacation time approaches. They'll take care of the pets for you, mow the lawn religiously, and honor their curfews—they say. Don't they realize we saw *Risky Business?* They go with us until they're twenty-one!

Once you realize any vacation is going to cost you a fortune, you might as well empty your bank account, fly off to an island, and go for the tan. Which is easier said than done, unless all your kids are in the same school. We can no longer find a week when they're all off together. If we do, there are no airline tickets available. I think our family vacation days are over. Once our youngest gets to college, my husband and I intend to see the world the way it was meant to be seen—without kids!

Family togetherness was so easy when they were young, Lord. Now, when we need it more than ever, it seems to be impossible. And yet there are evenings when we linger over the dinner table . . . car rides to relatives' . . . holiday gatherings. Teach us not to waste these times in bickering or correcting or lecturing, but to make them times of sharing and communion that bring us closer as a family.

And be ye kind one to another, tenderhearted, forgiving one another, even as God for Christ's sake hath forgiven you.

Ephesians 4:32

12

Messages

Teenagers aren't always home (thank heavens), but quite often mothers are, which makes us unautomated answering services. Most of the messages that baffle me come in ten minutes after I've drifted off to sleep. I can't turn on the light, put on my glasses, and write the message down without waking up Bill and sending him after paper and pencil, so things get garbled. Or maybe they were garbled in the first place.

*　　*　　*

"Hi, Mrs. Sortor. Please tell Laura I can't pick her up, but she has to be on the corner of Main and First at exactly seven-twenty-seven or we'll leave without her."

"Fine. Who is this?"

"She'll know." Click.

At 7:00 A.M. the next morning, the message will be relayed: "Someone—a girl, I think—called last night. She can't pick you up. Meet her on some street corner downtown around seven." Most of the time, she was able to fill in the gaps for herself.

*　　*　　*

"Mommy?"

"Yes?" I'm wide-awake. That word in that tone of voice wakes up any mother.

"I need help."

"Where are you?"

"Who is this?"

"Who's *this?*"

"Jane!"

I don't have a Jane. I don't even know a Jane. "Jane, I think you dialed the wrong number. Can I help you somehow?"

"You're not my mother."

"No. But I'll help if I can."

"*%#@)&!" Click.

That child needs more help than I could give her, anyway.

*   *   *

"Where's Jim?"

"Beats me. He left here after dinner."

"He was supposed to pick me up at work! If he comes in, tell him he's dead meat!" Click.

No. That's one I won't even bother passing on in the morning.

*   *   *

"I want a pepperoni pizza with extra cheese."

"Huh?"

"Pepperoni! Get it right this time, will ya?"

"Okay. Ten minutes." Click. ·

Now that was nasty of me. But our number is only one digit different from two local pizza parlors, and I'm tired of taking orders at 11:00 P.M. Especially rude ones. I hope it's still pouring when he goes in to collect his pizza!

*   *   *

"Steve?"

"No. Steve's asleep. Can I take a message?"

Giggle, giggle. Click.

I take the phone off the hook. This type of message is always repeated every ten minutes for at least an hour.

*   *   *

I finally decided I couldn't hack it anymore. I put the telephone on Bill's side of the bed. He wakes up easily, is immediately coherent, and is brusque enough to freeze the ear off anyone who dares to call after 11:00 P.M.

I'm sorry I'm a failure at this aspect of parenting, Lord. I don't do messages very well. Let my children understand this weakness in me. Let us all keep our patience.

He that sendeth a message by the hand of a fool cutteth off the feet, and drinketh damage.

Proverbs 26:6

13

Axioms:
Fourteen to Seventeen

The material on one book jacket is more than sufficient for a two-page book report.

Distance increases attraction: No teenager wants to date someone who goes to the same school.

Most families stop going out for dinner as soon as their children develop a taste for lobster.

The only person in the family qualified to put a new roll of toilet paper in the holder is Mother.

Check the children's bath for your shampoo *before* you get in the shower.

In any snowstorm, your son will be out shoveling other driveways for cash when you need to get out of the garage.

No teenager uses the same towel twice; three teens produce six towels on the bathroom floor daily.

The month you buy your son a new sports jacket is the month he'll grow three inches.

If your son has a suit that fits for Christmas, he won't have a shirt. If he has a shirt, he won't have a belt. If he has a belt, he'll wear white socks and sneakers with his suit.

A boy capable of rebuilding a carburetor is not necessarily capable of making his bed.

Any teen worth his salt can watch MTV and study chemistry at the same time.

14
Freshmen

Remember the first day of your freshman year in high school? Remember leaving home feeling like a big shot and coming home feeling like a toad? It's still the same.

In our town, kids go from kindergarten through eighth

grade in the same school. They know all the teachers, the quirks of each individual water fountain, and which rest rooms to stay out of. It's a small, secure world by the time they hit eighth grade.

Then they switch to a regional high school serving five area towns. A school that's spread out over an acre or more, with endless hallways and lockers that play musical chairs at night. A school filled with boys whose voices have already changed and girls wearing clothing that would have gotten them sent home from grammar school. Suddenly, instead of being a wise old veteran, your child is young, inexperienced, and slightly scared.

If your son is confused enough to ask an upperclassman the way to his algebra class, he's sure to end up in woodshop. He may even buy an elevator pass for two dollars—a good deal, he's assured. It might be, but our high school doesn't have an elevator—or a second floor!

High school freshmen also have transportation problems to contend with. Most of them live too close to school to qualify for a bus ride and too far to walk on a snowy day. Your son can't ride his bicycle to high school; it's just not done. He's too young to ride with upperclassmen who have cars (besides, none of them will acknowledge his existence), and he's too old to ride with you. Most of the time, he'll hoof it, unless the weather's unreasonable. Then he'll ask you to drop him a block away from the school.

After nine years of coming home at noontime for a nutritious lunch, your son now discovers the joys of the cafeteria lunch. The first week, all goes well. He can actually choose what he wants for lunch and buy goodies you never let him eat at home. Pizza for lunch! The freedom masks the taste. By the end of the second week, he's tried everything the free lunch offers—you couldn't ask more of a saint—and is buying peanut butter sandwiches or salads. He hates salads. Peanut butter makes him break out. By the third week, he's realized that mystery meat appears every Thursday, rain or shine. By the fourth, he's begging you to pack a lunch for him— *anything* will do!

His lunch period comes anytime between 10:30 A.M. and 2:00 P.M., depending on how the scheduling computer feels about his last name. No one in his right mind can face cafeteria food at 10:30 A.M., and by 2:00 P.M. whatever's left on the steam table is unrecognizable. If your son gets lucky enough to be scheduled into a noontime lunch period, the lines are so long that his lunch period's over before he gets to the food. It's good practice for him, in case he ever has to buy himself lunch in midtown Manhattan.

Somehow, he survives it. He finds old friends and makes new ones. He learns to pack his own lunches at 7:30 A.M. (Some mothers actually do this for their children. I tend to develop morning sickness if faced with bologna before noon.) He memorizes his locker's location and combination and learns to get from the east wing to the west wing in three minutes in heavy traffic and still manage to copy someone's homework on the way. The whole process makes him a little testy around the house for a good month, though. You just have to remember what it was like when you went through it and be understanding until it blows over.

Father, I still have nightmares about not being able to find my locker, so I guess those first few weeks of high school really were hard. Help my son through this period of adjustment. Keep his sense of humor in working order until he gets it all sorted out and finds the routine.

But made his own people to go forth like sheep, and guided them in the wilderness like a flock. And he led them on safely, so that they feared not. . . .

Psalms 78:52, 53

15 Homework

This is a nasty subject, but it has to be faced sometime.

I know parents whose children actually enjoy school, do their homework promptly, and bring home test results in the ninety-ninth percentile. These fortunate parents have only daughters, no sons. They are constitutionally incapable of understanding what the parents of boys are going through. They think you're doing something dreadfully wrong and have a hard time not looking smug. They're sometimes hard to like.

I can say that because I've been one of them. I sat on a tiny chair outside my daughter's classroom on parent-teacher conference day and saw the parents of boys come out of that room. They were easy to spot, with their red faces, set lips, defiant eyes, and clenched fists. Sometimes, Daddy had been dragged in to share the abuse; those parents came out either snapping at each other or murderously silent.

I felt smug. I was going in to hear compliments. *I* knew how to raise children!

Then Jim and Steve went to school. Both of them are every bit as intelligent as Laura, who continued merrily on her way as a model student requiring no motivation from me.

The boys did fine until about second grade, when they realized they were really expected to *work* in school. All those dittos they brought home in their packs were meant to be filled in, not used as ballast. Teachers got unpleasant when projects were assigned and blithely ignored. One of the boys had difficulty learning to read; the other learned, then vowed never to do it again. The one who couldn't read well was good at math but didn't think it necessary that his teacher should be able to decipher his answers. He'd done the math; grading it was *her* problem.

We tried everything. We took away everything but food and shelter without visible effect. We reasoned, we spanked, we yelled, we prayed. It didn't matter how much they liked their teachers, they still wouldn't do their homework or exert themselves more than was required to pass the grade.

Soon enough, I was the red-faced parent coming out of the parent-teacher conference. I wanted to kick the chair out from under that waiting parent of daughters who was trying not to laugh at me!

At first, you take the blame. You promise to do better, to spend the evenings working with your son on his reading, to motivate and encourage him at every opportunity. But it doesn't work, and the guilt keeps piling up on top of you until every evening is ruined by arguments about school.

After a few years, you learn how to handle it. For the rest of your son's school days, teachers are going to try to heap this guilt on you. They're going to continue to hint, ever so gently, that with a little more parental interest and concern, your son would begin to "work up to his potential."

Nonsense! Don't take it. Listen politely, nod understandingly, say thank you, but refuse to pick up that guilt and take it home. It's not yours. If it's anyone's it's your son's, and he gets his share every day at school and home. Once they get to fifth or sixth grade, your sons know exactly what they're doing (or not doing). They've made a conscious choice to be this way, and there's next to nothing you can do about it.

When they hit high school, I sat them down and washed my hands of it. No more checking their homework. No more reminding them about deadlines. I put them on notice that from then on, they sank or swam on their own. It was their life, their responsibility—not mine—and if they wanted to go to college, they'd shape up on their own.

It worked. They didn't turn into *A* students (eight years of neglect are hard to overcome), but they learned to monitor their own work and get *B*s and *C*s instead of *C*s and *D*s. I shrugged off all those years of guilt encrusted on my back and started performing my most vital duty: enjoying my children.

Why is it so hard for us to transfer responsibility to our children, Lord? We remember them as babies needing protection, instead of seeing them as individuals who should be responsible for their own actions. Help us turn over the reins when it's time and have faith in the abilities of our own children.

My son, be wise, and make my heart glad, that I may answer him that reproacheth me.

Proverbs 27:11

16 Fourteen

My children didn't have hobbies—they had obsessions. Our first son's obsession was models. From the age of fourteen until he went off to college, his bedroom ceiling was festooned with airplanes and satellites; every flat surface displayed battle cruisers.

I didn't mind. For one thing, it prevented me from dusting his room. When I tried, I would invariably break off some critical model piece and be told to leave the dusting to him. Gladly! Once a year I'd lug a bucket up to his room and dunk each model into it in an attempt to maintain some sanitary standards. A lot of decals ended up at the bottom of my pail, but if I was careful, he never noticed.

We were given permission to repaint his room the fall he left for college. Each model was carefully unhooked from the ceiling, given a dunking, and packed away in huge garbage bags. Each cuphook was taken out of the ceiling and its hole spackled into oblivion. The psychedelic posters came down for storage. We painted every structural surface of that room, washed the windows, remade the bed. The room sparkled. But it wasn't Jim's room anymore—it could have been a motel room, for all its personality.

Over Thanksgiving vacation, a Corvette poster reappeared in its normal place on the wall, along with two little mirrors. The battle cruisers are back on the dresser. Maybe over Christmas vacation he'll decorate a little more. I hope so. I like to go up to his room when I get lonely and look at what's important to him, even if it's only clutter.

Father, I know You can see through the clutter of my life, straight down to the person I really am. Help me do that for my children, too. I get tied up in dirty clothes too often. I see the bad exam mark and ignore the child behind it. I yell at the missed curfew before I listen to the explanation. Remind me that these frustrating things are not my child, any more than the person who yells too soon is really me. Focus my eyes on what's important when I see only the clutter on the surface.

My little children, let us not love in word, neither in tongue; but in deed and in truth.

1 John 3:18

17

The Good Old Days

The next time you find yourself lecturing your teens about the good old days and see their eyes begin to glaze over, take time to really remember those days. Things are different today, but a lot of things are also better.

In my youth it wasn't uncommon—or at least it wasn't shocking—for a girl to marry at fourteen or fifteen and have her first child six months later. A lot of girls just never came back for their sophomore year of high school. Families of twelve or fourteen children were considered a bit excessive, but there were quite a few of them around.

Boys who acted up in school, smoked, or spat in public—the kind who would be in counseling today, at worst—routinely found themselves before a judge offering two choices: Join the navy or go to prison.

Almost everyone over the age of sixteen worked after school and weekends, which was fine, except that the money they earned was usually turned over to their parents to help pay the rent. The lucky ones earned fifty cents an hour; baby-sitters made twenty-five cents an hour.

Most kids never made it out of town. Only a few went to college, and those who did usually went to nearby state teachers' colleges. If you couldn't afford that and were determined to make something of yourself and see the world, you joined the army or navy. There weren't many other choices.

Some young family men commuted to work in the mills and factories thirty miles away and made decent money that way. But commuting was not considered natural or normal in those days, and thirty miles on local roads made for a long, dangerous commute.

These are not depression times we're talking about, either. This was postwar America, when things were just beginning to boom. But the boom hadn't quite reached my town yet.

Were we more moral and respectful then than our children are now? Only on the surface. Only because we had no other choice. A lot of the girls who didn't "fool around" didn't because they were scared, not always because of their high moral standards. Boys were well behaved and respectful of their elders because they were scared of them or prone to seasickness. We were well behaved in school because a call from the principal meant a good licking at home.

It wasn't totally oppressive, of course. All in all, it was a nice town to grow up in, with nice people living in it. And although you couldn't get rich there, you were safe and cared for and loved.

We were "good kids," but the truth is, a good kid of today is really a better person than we were, because we were basically good out of fear. Some things are better now than in the good old days.

Keep me from self-righteousness when I speak to my teenagers, Lord. Help me remember my own teenage years truthfully, not turning them into some golden age, when I was actually as willful and confused then as my children are today.

So teach us to number our days, that we may apply our hearts unto wisdom.

Psalms 90:12

18 Church

Somewhere along the way, I stopped forcing my teens to go to church. It didn't seem like something that should be forced. By the time they hit fourteen or fifteen, I felt it should be their decision, not mine.

Being teenagers, they chose not to go—not directly, anyway. One of them did attend a youth group at a friend's church. He knew all the kids there, and they had a good time together. Another went to church with her boyfriend. It wasn't our church, but it was church, and I counted it. I have a feeling the Lord is going to get them yet.

I know a lot of people can't be this casual about the subject and will say I've let my kids down on it. They may very well be right; it does worry me. But raising teenagers is a process of letting go, of not trying to force your beliefs on people old enough to be forming their own. This is a decision that's between them and God now. I trust them; I also trust God. Somewhere along the way, in His own good time, they'll work things out between them, even if I never know about it.

Lord, this is a decision I can't make for them, any more than I can tell them they're going to be doctors or engineers. On these life decisions I can only tell them how I feel and hope for the best. This one is in Your hands. I can't think of a better place for it.

The Lord is not slack concerning his promise, as some men count slackness; but is longsuffering to us-ward, not willing that any should perish, but that all should come to repentance.

2 Peter 3:9

19

Bedtime

Every fall, we'd have a dinnertime conversation along these lines:

"Mom, can I stay up later this year?"

"How much later?"

"Until midnight?"

"On school nights? That's too late."

"No, on weekends."

"It's too late then, too."

"*Everyone* stays up that late! I'm not a baby anymore, you know."

Every year, year after year, for every child; it tires you out.

By the time they were freshmen in high school, I gave in and suspended supervision of their weekend bedtimes. (We're not talking about curfews, here. That's another thing altogether.) At that age, they could outlast me, anyway. They'd find me slumped and snoring in front of the TV and send me to bed so they could watch "Saturday Night Live."

Going to bed while your children are still up is a big hurdle in your life. It's unnatural. You lie there fighting sleep, your mind filled with questions: Will they remember to let the dog out? Will they lock up? Will they sneak a dozen friends in and have a wild party while you doze? The answers are yes, yes, and no. You didn't raise a bunch of idiots.

Besides, our kids knew that while I slept like the dead, my husband heard *everything*. He counted the number of times the refrigerator opened each night (fifteen—five for each child). No matter how they tried, no child of ours ever sneaked upstairs without his father hearing. He knew how many people under twenty-one were in the house at all times. And he wonders why he's so tired in the mornings!

Once you let your children choose their own weekend bedtimes, the weekdays are soon beyond your control. I personally think anyone under eighteen should be in bed by eleven on school nights, but they have to test you. They'll stay up until 2:00 A.M. watching movies they hate, just because they can. Their whole first week of freedom will be lived in a daze of exhaustion. You'll get notes from teachers and calls from other parents who want to know if your child can *really* stay up all night if he wants to. Tell them it's temporary, because it is. As soon as he's flexed his nighttime muscles, the average high-school-age child will resume going to bed at a reasonable hour on school nights.

I gave my kids this particular freedom as training for us all. I knew the time was rapidly coming when I'd have to let go on more important things, so I practiced letting go with bedtimes. They practiced being responsible for the health of their own bodies.

As of now, I don't know when they return to a normal waking-sleeping pattern. Mine haven't. My college-age son stays up until 4:00 A.M. and sleeps until 2:00 P.M. when he's home from college. (I don't want to know what he does *at* college.) Another is a 2:00 A.M. to 11:00 A.M. sleeper on weekends. The third is generally in bed by midnight and up by nine on weekends, but that's only because he doesn't have his driver's license yet. This freedom doesn't seem to have damaged them in any way, so they're welcome to it. But are they ever in for a shock when they have their own babies and face 2:00 A.M. feedings!

Why do parents have such a hard time with their children's bedtimes, Lord? It's instinctive, I think, left over from our cave-dwelling, saber-toothed-tiger days. Or is it that I just don't want to let go yet? Whatever the reason, teach me to trust them a little more each day as they grow and mature, as You trust me with my own decisions. What I ask of You, I should gracefully give to my own children.

When thou liest down, thou shalt not be afraid: yea, thou shalt lie down, and thy sleep shall be sweet.

Proverbs 3:24

20 Fifteen

In our state, a fifteen-year-old is recognized as a responsible adult by the Department of Motor Vehicles: He can drive a moped. On the road. With sleepy commuters and overloaded trucks and seventeen-year-olds in crowded cars with bad brakes.

It gives you food for thought. Who says a kid who doesn't need to shave yet should be let loose on the road? How can a boy who can't control his voice control a moped that goes forty miles an hour? Obviously no one in the Department of Motor Vehicles ever had a fifteen-year-old!

If you're lucky, your child will turn fifteen in the late fall or early winter and you can hold him off until spring. You just have to pray for a cold, snowy winter to reduce the howls of outrage to bearable levels.

Buying the moped is the easiest part, hundreds of them being available from seventeen-year-olds who just got their car licenses. Of course, no one can tell the difference between a good and bad moped, so you'll probably buy a lemon (75 percent of them are natural lemons). To even the odds, insist on the helmet being part of the deal.

Come spring, you'll have to go through the licensing ordeal: standing in lines for manuals, permits, and written tests. Then you get to load the moped into the station wagon and drive your child fifteen miles for his road test. *Note:* A five-year-old could pass a moped road test, so don't hold out any hope he'll fail.

At first we only let our boys drive locally during daylight hours. That worked fine until daylight saving time and school closing set them free. Then they were gone.

And I mean *gone:* mobile . . . on their own . . . with the whole county to explore . . . in the ugly leather jackets we couldn't really complain about because they'd bought them with their own money and their bodies needed the protection.

We couldn't go to bed until the moped was in the garage, which caused other problems: His curfew was earlier than he wanted, and we didn't get enough sleep on weekends. It's not that you can't physically or morally go to sleep—it's that half the time you'll doze off just before he wakes you to pick him up (and you never know which half). Mopeds break down a lot. Usually on rainy nights in strange towns—towns you wouldn't have allowed him to be in, if you'd known he was going. By the way, mopeds do not fit into sedans. They don't fit into anything smaller than a Jeep or van, and even then it's a struggle to keep them from spilling gas all over the inside of the vehicle.

All mopeds do is free you from driving your child around every day of your life until he gets his driver's license. Since driving a fifteen-year-old around is not one of life's little pleasures, that's one big factor in their favor. It doesn't begin to balance out the worry you'll live through, though. Hold out, if you're strong!

It must be confusing being my child, Lord. I can be so reasonable about some things, and so unreasonable about others! Do they know that reason has very little to do with it? That fear is often the deciding factor? I've often asked You to help me understand them, Lord, but it's also important that You help them understand me. Help them be patient when I can't explain my decisions. Help them understand that besides being their mother, I am also a normal, emotional, vulnerable person.

And he said unto them, Why are ye so fearful? how is it that ye have no faith?

Mark 4:40

21 Early Dating

Dating sneaks up on parents and blindsides them when they're feeling safe and complacent.

From their early teens, your children are hidden in the middle of a group that floats from house to house, pizza parlor to youth group, one amorphous organism with multiple mouths and feet. To you, they all look and act the same. Sometimes this organism is composed of only one sex; sometimes both are represented. But it's an asexual group, with no obvious couples—just a bunch of friends systematically ravaging the neighborhood refrigerators. If you drive them to the bowling alley, the boys sit in one seat, the girls in another. Nothing to worry about, right?

Watch out; it's a trap. They're just lulling you into a false sense of security, biding their time like any good guerrilla group. One evening you'll pick them up from the bowling alley and discover the old seating arrangement has been scrapped. With much quiet pushing and shoving, they're contriving to seat themselves in your basic boy-girl arrangement, in an overloaded car that leaves little room for social niceties. The next time you draw car duty, half the group will be waiting for you in shadowy spots far removed from the rest of the giggling group. Shortly thereafter, *no one* will be waiting on the curb for you, necessitating a bit of yelling and horn blowing to assemble the chicks.

By now it should have dawned on you that these kids, although they seem to be part of the old group, are actually dating—and you haven't set down the house dating rules yet. You've been outflanked.

You were going to tell your son he couldn't date until he's sixteen, and now you're flushing him out of the shadows where he's trying to lock braces with a girl who could beat him to a pulp five years ago.

Don't panic yet. If you keep your head, you'll see they're all dating within the old group. They still all go out together, but in a constantly changing kaleidoscope pattern of couples. The girl with the braces is replaced by a blonde, who gives way to the brain of the group, who moves on to leave your befuddled but happy son with her best friend. As long as you can see no pattern to it, you still have time (*see* "The Talk").

Boys seem to have it easier than girls during this stage. Girls take it so personally! Each boyfriend is perfect, just what she's been looking for, so mature and sweet and gentle (this is your son they're talking about?). He's perfect until he smiles his special smile at her best friend and breaks her heart. Girls sit by the phone and wait for a special boy to call them, until it's obvious that the message relayed by a mutual friend didn't do its job. Girls weep and sigh and contrive to collect pictures and mementos that they then proceed to ceremoniously burn the following week, setting off the smoke alarm at 2:00 A.M. It's hard being a fifteen-year-old girl.

On the other hand, being a fifteen-year-old boy is pretty rewarding. It's always nice, being an object of devotion. The mysterious crank phone calls get to be a drag, but they do indicate that someone out there cares enough to reach out and hang up. Suddenly your clumsy son, who trips over the dog in broad daylight and never knows where his sneakers are, has become a person of worth. He starts to shave once a week. He borrows your husband's after-shave whether he shaves or not. He gets his hair styled instead of going to the neighborhood barber. He no longer walks; now he swaggers. Yes, being a fifteen-year-old boy is very rewarding.

Let him enjoy it. Next year he'll really begin to care about someone and get his little macho heart broken, because boys don't take dating personally until they're sixteen. This undoubtedly has more to do with part-time jobs and cash-flow problems than it does with hormones. Whatever the reason, dating has come into your child's life far too early—as far as you're concerned.

Life's about to get complicated around here, isn't it, Father? I want my child to grow up and know love and all its joys—but not just yet. He's still mostly boy. Teach me to be helpful as he goes through this transition into manhood. Guide him, protect him, keep his heartbreaks bearable.

. . . be thou strong therefore, and shew thyself a man; And keep the charge of the Lord thy God, to walk in his ways . . . that thou mayest prosper in all that thou doest, and whithersoever thou turnest thyself.

1 Kings 2:2, 3

22

Numbers

I just figured this out: By the time my youngest is 20, I will have had a teenager in the house for 13 consecutive years. That boggles my mind. Bank robbers serve less time than that.

At the other end of the scale, I had a baby in diapers from 1965 to 1974. Nine years of changing, what? nine diapers a day? That's 29,565 diapers in the course of my life. Not counting grandchildren still to come.

Then there's college from 1983 to 1995: 12 years at $15,000 a year, which includes everything from tuition to telephone bills. I multiplied that out for you: $180,000. I don't *have* $180,000. How are we doing this?

What other fun things can we calculate? Parent-teacher conferences from kindergarten through high school: 13 years × 2 a year × 3 kids = 78 conferences. Think of the books I could have read in that time.

Want to really feel like a martyr? Number of meals cooked from 1965 (birth of first child) to 1991 (age 20 of last child): 3 × 365 × 26 years = 28,470. Very close to the number of diapers changed, isn't it?

Number of years with a teenage driver in the house: 9. Number of Saturday nights spent worrying: 468. Number of hours of sleep lost worrying: 936.

Number of times I've told a boy between the ages of 15 and 19 to mow the lawn once a week for 5 months of each year: 6 years × 5 months × 4.3 weeks = 129 cuttings × 3 threats per cutting = 387 times.

Loads of laundry done from the birth of the first child to age 20 of the last child: 2 a day × 365 × 26 years = 18,980. I take some holidays off, but make up by doing 4 loads the next day.

Number of evenings spent supervising homework: 180 school days a year × 12 years × 3 kids = 6,480 evenings of frustration.

You could go on for a long time, doing this. The point is, parenting involves a lot of time, effort, and cash. More than you realize until some wiseguy figures it out for you. And if you begin to feel a little tired as your last child becomes a teenager, maybe you've got a right.

Most of the time, a parent doesn't count, she just does. That's the way You made us, Father, and it's a good thing. When I get a little tired or frustrated, remind me this is how it should be, that You appreciate my efforts and honor my work.

The Lord recompense thy work, and a full reward be given thee of the Lord God of Israel, under whose wings thou art come to trust.

Ruth 2:12

23
Curfews

First off, you have to define the word *curfew* to a teenager. With this whole subject, you have to be very specific, leaving no room for interpretation or misunderstanding.

Curfew is the time a teenager comes home. That means inside the house, with no visitors, with the door locked and the outside lights turned off. It doesn't mean coming in, turning off the lights, locking the door, and sneaking back out for another two hours. It doesn't mean bringing back six friends who have later curfews, so you won't die of boredom or embarrassment. It doesn't even mean coming in and ordering a pizza to be delivered and enjoyed in solitude. It means no incoming telephone calls (outgoing calls may be allowed in some families). Curfew is the end of socialization.

No wonder they fight it. A teenager who can't socialize during every waking hour is miserable. And oppressed. And misunderstood. Tough. Parents have the right to peace of mind for a few hours a day, which is precisely why curfews were invented.

The easiest and most effective curfew ever invented is "One-half hour after the dance (party) ends." That's verifiable and not open to successful argument. But they soon reach the age where they're not going to formal dances, dinners, or parties. They just go "out." They "hang out" at McDonald's or Burger King, moving on when the police begin giving them the fisheye. They slouch around family rooms belonging to other teenagers, moving on to another when the parents run out of food or begin giving them the fisheye. They move in schools, like restless mackerel—first here, then there—untraceable for hours.

You finally have to admit it: You do not know where your child is at 10:00 P.M.

The latest we ever got to with formal curfews was midnight, which was generally the year before they got their driver's license. The first year of their license, we had a gentleman's agreement that one o'clock would be the latest they'd show up. It wasn't a cut-and-dried curfew. Sometimes they got away with being a little late; sometimes we asked them to be a little earlier or just refused to give them the car keys. We were practicing letting go again, and they were practicing being responsible and not making me worry. In our family, that's the greatest offense of all, and the most likely to cause unjust punishment. Don't make Mom worry!

Sometime during their senior year, curfews disappeared altogether. I could no longer stay awake long enough to know when they came home, but my light-sleeping husband generally knew, and he would make the appropriate noises if it was too late. Later on during that year, even he would cease to notice when the kids got in, and we would both sleep the sleep of the just and pray our kids knew what they were doing.

There are a few basic rules parents must remember about curfews:

1. *Curfews are made solely for the convenience of parents.* Society really doesn't care what time your teenager comes home. Your teenager cares, but he doesn't count. Set curfews you are comfortable with and don't pay any attention to what "everyone else" does.

2. *You have the right to change your mind.* If after much dickering and pleading, your teen convinces you he should be allowed out until one o'clock, then blows it with some totally irresponsible behavior, you are not stuck with one o'clock. *See* Rule 1.

3. *Teenagers need curfews.* Curfews allow boys to take rotten dates home early and blame it on you. They allow girls to leave the group and come home early without losing face. Many younger teens have been able to back away from trouble thanks to a curfew imposed by their unreasonable parents.

4. *Curfews are expendable.* When a teen shows he doesn't need a curfew, you have the right to do away with it. More than likely, you'll have to reimpose one within a week, but he'll love the trust and freedom while it lasts.

Somewhere near the end of high school, you'll find you really don't want a curfew anymore. Your child has grown into an adult along the way, and *you* feel uncomfortable with curfews. It's time to let go of one more thing and pray you've done your work well.

Lord of the night streets, my child's out there with You again, and I've put my trust in both You and him. Keep him wise and cautious, Lord, safe from harm and foolishness. He knows right from wrong—I must let him go out into that darkness with all the

faith of youth. But stay by his side, remind him of the lessons
we've taught him, bring him safely home.

Casting all your care upon him; for he careth for you.

1 Peter 5:7

24 Threats and Groundings

A parent has to be inventive when trying to motivate (read that as *punish*) a teenager. After all, he's been living with you for a good many years now; he's heard it all before. For instance:

1. "If you don't hang up and come eat your dinner, I'll tear that phone off the wall!" No teenager is fooled by this one. There is, after all, the very slight chance the next call might be for you. However, if you say it with just a touch of desperation in your voice, he'll hang up, rather than take the chance of being cut off from the world until the repairman arrives.

2. "Your clothes can sit there on the floor and *rot* before I'll pick them up!" Totally ineffective. He knows you can't

possibly vacuum around them and can't risk the health hazard of not vacuuming once a week.

3. "Pick up this room or I'll throw everything on the floor out!" An interesting ploy. It might work, if you actually do it once. *Note:* I did. It works for me

4. "Eat your vegetables or you get no dessert!" This stopped working when he hit thirteen. Now you're lucky to get him to eat any part of his meal. He can always hit McDonald's at 8:00 P.M.

5. "Cut that grass today or you get no allowance!" He made seventy-two dollars this week, working part-time. What does he need an allowance for?

As you can see, threats have limited effectiveness. You'll go on using them because you're human, but none of you will take them seriously. At best, they indicate to a teenager that you are getting serious, and sometimes that's all that's needed.

The biggest threat of all is ". . . or you're grounded!" As a threat, this, too, is limited. He can always take the chance that you won't follow through.

As an after-the-fact punishment, however, grounding is one of God's little gifts to parents. It works best when used very sparingly for the most serious of offenses. Always make it a surprise.

Your son knows what his curfew is; you tell him on his way out the door every evening. Being normal, he stretches it by fifteen minutes, then half an hour. He's testing. One night, he's going to push beyond your limit and be flagrantly, willfully late. This limit varies from parent to parent. I get worried at forty-five minutes; I panic and punish at one hour.

Don't say a thing when you hear him come in. Let him sleep the sleep of the forgiven and traipse downstairs innocently at eleven in the morning. Then, as you watch him eat cold pizza for breakfast, calmly say, "Oh, by the way, you're grounded for a week."

He, of course, will be all innocence. "Why? What did I do?"

At this point, I should warn you to define *grounded* for your son. There are various levels of grounding. Sometimes it means total isolation: no phone calls in or out, no trips out, no visitors in. That's a bread-and-water grounding, used for insubordination or willful acts of disobedience. For less serious offenses, he may still have use of the telephone. If you flew off the handle and were too harsh in your punishment, you may even let his friends in when they appear on your doorstep five minutes after the grounding. You have to get the rules straight each time.

Grounding is undeniably effective, but you have to live through it. Our daughter used to bargain her way through her sentences: "But I have to go to the library to do my science report! I promise I'll be back at nine." Sometimes she won, if she used the right tactics.

Our older son had the best technique I've ever seen. Instead of retiring to his room to sulk, he lived at my heels. I'd turn around from the kitchen sink and find him staring out the window. Sighing. I'd feel a presence in the living room while reading and look up to see him slumped against the doorjamb. Sighing. He followed me every-where, like a little lost puppy. Sighing. It was pathetic. It often got his sentence reduced by days!

So far our youngest has only been grounded once in his life (he learned a lot by watching his brother and sister). It was a justified one-week offense, but he was allowed the telephone because it was a "duty grounding" on my part. His brother had just served two weeks hard time for the same offense (done deliberately), so I had to punish Steve (who did it thoughtlessly). Sometimes it gets complicated, deciding who gets what for how long. I wonder who invented grounding? I'll have to check my Bible, but I bet it was Adam and Eve!

Father, I hate to have to punish my children at this age, but they have to know some things are just not allowed. Help me as I work my way through this duty. Give me good judgment; make me fair.

Correct thy son, and he shall give thee rest; yea, he shall give delight unto thy soul.

Proverbs 29:17

25   Music

I don't understand my teenagers' music, in many ways.

First, I literally do not understand it. I can sit in a teenager's room, listen to an entire album, and not understand one word of it. I can't tell where one word ends and another begins, assuming those were actual words amid the groans, screams, and yells. I've even sat there with the words printed out in front of me and heard absolutely no correlation between what I was reading and what I was hearing. Maybe they print the words just to throw parents off, and what's printed out is not what's actually on the record. It's just devious enough to be true.

I figured deafness had something to do with my inability to understand a record. I have a slight hearing loss, anyway, and as anyone with this problem knows, being yelled at is no help. So I turned the volume down and tried again, to no avail. Even when my teens interpreted for me, I couldn't hear the words. Very frustrating for a word person.

I don't understand MTV, either. You'd think that would be within the realm of understanding for someone who grew up on MGM musical extravaganzas, wouldn't you? But in my day, a smiling singer meant something nice was happening—they gave you little clues like that. With

MTV, there are no clues; nothing that's going on seems related to the song. Of course, since I can't understand the words, what do I know?

I'm willing to admit I haven't given MTV a fair chance. I think there's more to it than there was to my MGM musicals: more symbolism, maybe even a little more thought. But I'm too old to learn to appreciate a new art form now.

I do understand that music has an entirely different meaning for my kids than it did for me at that age. I'm a country music person—I like things simple and catchy and true to life. But my music doesn't *define* me. Lovers of classical music will still be my friends. I can go out to dinner with a soft-rock listener without coming to blows over the background music. I can even stand elevator-music people; I married one.

It doesn't work that way with teens. They *are* what they listen to. The first question a teen will be asked on his first day in a new school is, "What's your favorite group?" His answer will lump him in with everyone else liking the same group. He'll be expected to dress and act in accordance with that classification for the remainder of his school days. Even if he doesn't really fit in with the group (maybe he just threw out a name he thought they'd like), his music keeps him there. It influences his dating possibilities, the parties he's invited to, even the marks he's expected to get.

We had a system like that in my school, too, but it was based on which part of town you came from or how much money your father made. Come to think of it, maybe their system is better. My sons can change the music they listen to, but I couldn't move my family to a better part of town!

Music is far more important to them than it ever was to me. I wanted it in the background. They want it up front, inside them, part of the rhythm of their very lives. Music joins them, bonds them, defines them. Music gives them a place in their world and makes them secure. Music makes them different from adults, which is undoubtedly its main attraction.

I don't understand their music, but that's okay. Some things should remain private and unshared with your parents—a semisecret teen thing, like Pig Latin. *That* I can understand!

Lord, I don't approve of some of the music my child listens to, but he doesn't approve of mine, and I still listen to it. As long as I don't see it changing his life or his morals, as long as it's just a pleasure and not a temptation, I'll just have to learn to put up with it.

Praise the Lord with harp: sing unto him with the psaltery and an instrument of ten strings. Sing unto him a new song; play skilfully with a loud noise.

Psalms 33:2, 3

26 Friends

Teenage friendships are something special. Many teen friendships last a lifetime, through different colleges, marriages, children, into old age. I have friends I haven't seen in years, but when we do meet again, it'll be as if we've never been apart. I hope my children are as lucky in their friendships.

At the same time, there's nothing quite as wacky as a teenage friendship. One day your son is standing beside his friend, ready to take on all comers in some senseless teenage brawl. The next, he's begging you to say he's "not home" when his friend calls. The boy your daughter absolutely adores one day will be traded like a baseball card the next. And somehow, through all the ups and downs, the same group will remain friends for years.

I think it's like battlefield friendships: They may have discovered as they matured that they do not really like a guy, but they went through puberty together, so that makes them friends for life.

To me, it's a wonder a teenager has any friends at all. Ever hear a teenage boy on the phone with another?

"So? What'a you want? That's stupid! You dorf! Yeah . . . okay. I'll see you when I get there. Get off my back, will you?"

When you tell him that's no way to talk to a friend, he

looks at you as though you're from another planet. Then there are conversations with girlfriends:

"Hm. I suppose so. No! Maybe. I'll let you know." Ah, love!

The friends your children make in their early teens are different from the ones of their late teens. This doesn't mean they aren't the same kids—they're just different. In the early teens, all your daughter's short-lived boyfriends will look alike. Worse yet, none of them will be able to talk to you. None of your son's friends will willingly talk to him in the house if you're present; they go out to the driveway, sit on the hood of your car, scratching the paint a little, and freeze. No matter how welcome you try to make them feel, you are obviously the Enemy.

It gets better as they get older. One day your daughter will bring home a boy capable of constructing a complete sentence. He'll laugh at your husband's bad jokes and stay for dinner. You'll actually come to like the kid. *Hint:* This is probably the one you should keep an eye on!

Your son and his friends will pick at the roast beef you were saving for tomorrow's dinner and take over the kitchen until 2:00 A.M. In a matter of months, your house will be overrun with starving teenagers, their music, their laughter. Some will even sit and talk with you, as long as you forgo giving unsolicited advice.

I loved it. They were loud, but I knew where they were. They were rude to one another, but never to me. They ate and drank up about a hundred dollars' worth of food a week, but I knew what they were drinking. They brought along girlfriends and turned out the lights. I gave them precisely long enough for a good kiss, coughed as I approached the room, and turned the lights back on. They beat me in games of Ping-Pong and lost to my husband. They talked to us about colleges and careers and cars.

My son's in college now. I miss him. I also miss his friends and can't wait until they all come home for Thanksgiving vacation.

Sometimes I think my own children are more than enough, Lord. Most of the time, I prefer them and all their friends. But there are times . . . ! Keep me hospitable, please. Keep me patient when they drink all the milk at 10:00 P.M. or keep me awake when we should all be asleep. Make my house a home where they feel welcome at any time, whatever their needs. Give me the grace to be a help to those who ask for it—and to keep my opinions to myself when not asked!

. . . that now at this time your abundance may be a supply for their want, that their abundance also may be a supply for your want. . . .

2 Corinthians 8:14

Lord, Don't You Get Frustrated With Teenagers Too?

27

"I'm Reading"

It always surprises me to find one of my children reading. In this multimedia age, reading is becoming a lost art, like letter writing; a reader is a member of an endangered species.

No one could accuse my kids of being bookworms, by any means, but if I'm making a trip to the bookstore, I can always find at least one child willing to join me. Especially if I'm treating.

The last time I went, Steven came along to buy some required summer reading and look for a book he hasn't been able to find yet—part of a series that apparently died on its publisher. (I have to find that book for him. It's important.) On the way home, we discussed science-fiction authors, past and present. I gave him some names, he gave me some in return, and we found we'd both been captivated by some of the same writers. It was a conversation I hadn't expected, a surprise blessing.

My other son, who's never been a fast reader, carries a book in his car to nibble at little by little and replace with another one when it's done. My daughter and I share some books, leaving them in the living room with two bookmarks in them at once and scrupulously not discussing the plot until we're both done.

Don't get the wrong impression here. They don't walk around with books in their hands or try to read during dinner, like I used to at their ages. Reading is pretty low on their list of priorities. But even teenagers have occasional times when there's nothing to do, and on a rainy weekend, they will pick up a book out of boredom.

If I feel it's been too long since any of them looked at a printed page, I can always make them go on a family vacation with us. Take a teenager a hundred miles away from his friends and deposit him in a poor-reception area for television, and you've created an instant reader! It's sneaky, but it works.

I still give each of them a new book every Christmas, as I have since they were born. Some get read, some don't. At least they'll have something to put on their bookshelves when they move into their own places.

Reading's important to me. Someday it may be to them, too, but the point is, I've never *told* one of them how important I think it is to read. They've picked up on it because they see us reading every day. And I thought all those afternoons I'd spent immersed in a book were selfish times. I didn't know I was teaching them anything, but I was.

Father, even when I'm not thinking about it, I seem to be teaching through my actions. Make those actions worthy lessons that will be helpful to my children, not harmful.

For I have given you an example, that ye should do as I have done to you.

John 13:15

28 Sixteen

I'm a strong believer in reality parenting, as opposed to ostrich parenting. No matter how much more simple it would be, things are *not* the same as when we were kids, and we have to live in the here and now with our children.

I hear more parents complain about the early teen years than about the later ones, but it's the later ones that hurt. It's easy to accept a thirteen-year-old's refusal to get a haircut. You can recognize it as a normal growth process and simply refuse to be seen in public with him. But when your sixteen-year-old absolutely refuses to talk to you for no discernible reason, you're into real pain.

A mother may react to a child's unjustified shunning in several ways. She may sit him down for a "good talk" (one-sided, of course), explain that she knows his silence is a natural form of teenage rebellion, and tell him she understands. (I personally don't understand this type of parent, but whatever works for you is fine by me.) On the other hand, it's perfectly normal to get mad and do a little judicious stomping around yourself when this happens. Or you can browbeat your husband into "talking to your son about respecting his mother," a tactic that is guaranteed to get *two* men mad at you.

I stumbled onto a two-pronged approach: I insisted on common civility at all times and left him in his silence whenever possible. I didn't enjoy it, but I could live with it, and since an ignored rebellion is a boring rebellion, he got over it. He'd made his point that he didn't have to talk to anyone unless he wanted to, and I'd admitted that was his right, as long as he was polite about it. Sometimes reality is silent.

Another reality is that from the age of sixteen on, your child is a party animal. It does no good to ask where he's going, although you keep trying. He may be facing some of the things you'd hoped you could avoid a little longer. Well, you're not invited, so how do you deal with it?

All I've ever been able to do is clearly state our beliefs— as often as possible, in as many ways as possible, without "lecturing"—and pray a lot. Your child's been living with you for sixteen years, after all. He's not dumb; he knows what you believe in. Now it's up to him to accept or reject your principles, and you can't *force* a sixteen-year-old to accept anything.

So your daughter's going to come home with a hickey now and then, or her date will be unable to meet your gaze when he picks her up. Be realistic. Tell her how you feel about premarital sex and why. A naive parent is absolutely no help to a teenager, and knowing about something does not necessarily mean making use of it. I know how to climb a fifty-foot ladder, but it's not something I'm ever going to do!

It's impossible for me to be "reasonable" about drugs, though. I try not to rant or rave, but I still end up saying, "Never. Absolutely *never!*" At least they know I mean it.

The horrible truth is, they know kids on drugs, and they don't really need my warnings. I hear the tone in their voices when they say, "He's a druggie," or, "He's a waste product." It says, "He's dead," and although it breaks my heart to hear them say that about a child their own age, I thank God they recognize the danger. You see, this world has forced our children to become realists, too.

Lord, I don't like some of the things my children do, but I still love my children. I can no longer keep the world from them; it would be foolish to try. Make them strong, Lord. If what we've tried to teach them is right, they'll remember it, and it will help them make their own life choices.

Only take heed to thyself, and keep thy soul diligently, lest thou forget the things which thine eyes have seen, and lest they depart from thy heart all the days of thy life: but teach them thy sons, and thy sons' sons.

Deuteronomy 4:9

29

The Talk

How can you write about teenagers without mentioning sex? I suppose you could, but it would be a cop-out, and if there's one thing a parent can't do, it's cop out.

Remember how embarrassing it was when your kids were about four and began asking questions? I stammered and stuttered, read books of advice on how to answer those questions, and somehow got through it. By the time they were teens, I'd finally collected my wits and figured out all the answers, but by then, no one was asking any questions!

You can sit around a long time, waiting for a teenager to ask questions about sex. Right up until he gets married and makes you a grandparent, as a matter of fact. You may assume this lack of questions implies either a lack of interest or an already-existing fund of knowledge; both are highly dangerous assumptions. If you assume he's not interested, you're only fooling yourself. If you assume he already knows everything, you may be right, but what he "knows" may not be.

Schools do teach the rudiments of sexuality nowadays, but you can't depend on that. Maybe your son had a question about something in health class. Do you really think he would raise his hand in front of all the other guys and risk making a fool of himself? Besides, schools don't get into the important stuff until twelfth grade—far too late for most kids.

No, you have to assume, by sixteen at the latest, that he's *very* interested and knows absolutely nothing reliable. Which means you have to sit him down for The Talk. Or, if that is absolutely beyond your capabilities (and don't feel bad if it is), present him with a good book, make sure he reads it, then ask for questions or have a pop quiz. This is one assigned book you can be sure he'll read, at least.

It's not that hard to run through the actual facts themselves. You sort of detach your mind from your emotions, take a deep breath, and do it, like diving into a cold swimming pool on a hot day. Most parents sound a bit like an auctioneer during this phase.

Once he's got the facts straight, you'll be tempted to call it quits, but you know you can't. You also have some very important opinions you need to convey, and since you're both already totally embarrassed, you might as well forge ahead. It'll be weeks before he'll dare to sit down alone with you again, anyway.

So do it: Tell him your beliefs and your hopes for him, what your faith teaches, what you expect of him. Because all the facts in the world are useless unless they're put into perspective. Finally you can let him go and take a long walk to stop your hands from shaking.

As hard as The Talk is, it's really the easy part. At least it's over with pretty fast. The hard part's in the living. The subject's going to come up again, time after time—in the form of curfews, acceptable dates, accountability, and daily activities. Just keep making your beliefs known, one day at a time as the opportunities present themselves, and you'll do fine. You do get used to it, after a while, but by the time you do, your second child will be ready for The Talk—and that's no easier the second time around!

This is important stuff, Lord, so help me teach my child what he has to know. Don't let embarrassment make me avoid this subject. Let me teach him thoroughly and with love.

And all thy children shall be taught of the Lord; and great shall be the peace of thy children.

Isaiah 54:13

30 Work

At sixteen, a child decides between school sports and work. In some cases it's an easy decision; I suspect most McDonald's are full of uncoordinated sixteen-year-olds with no hopes of an athletic scholarship from any college. Others (especially boys) would rather be able to afford to date now or save money for college, instead of sacrificing their bodies for school spirit; so they join the work force. Some manage to do it all, but I never had one of them.

We've historically been a McDonald's family. Two of our kids can now swab down a tile floor and clean out any grease pit they may stumble upon in the future. McDonald's taught them one thing they couldn't learn from me: They are now willing to suffer through four years of college to avoid a lifetime of unskilled labor. Our youngest is determined to avoid smelling like a hamburger and is studying to be a lifeguard. He's decided that sitting on a high chair in view of all the girls in town has definite advantages over standing over a hot grill six hours a day. We're letting him enjoy his illusions while he can; I don't think he intends to be a professional lifeguard, anyway.

Working was good for them. My daughter learned the skill of serving the hungry public. The serving was easy to learn, but being polite to rude, obnoxious adults was hard. What makes people treat working teenagers with such disrespect? Do they treat their own children that way? She coped, learning a lot about life and work that will help her for the rest of her working days. She also met the best boyfriend a mother could hope for at McDonald's.

My son overcame his macho fear of cooking at McDonald's. He's invaluable at neighborhood barbeques—the fastest spatula in the East. Once he learned the basics of food handling, he moved on to stock work at the A&P, which was *the* place to work that year and paid fifty cents more an hour. His main claim to fame lies in his summer work at a local cemetery. He's the only lawn mower in the county who can run a Sensation full tilt through a patch of poison ivy without suffering one itch. It's a valuable skill that gets him his job back every summer. He enjoys working there, but has learned not to say exactly where he works; instead, he calls himself a landscaper and avoids a lot of "Ooh!"s.

I'm all for a teenager working part-time, as long as he has the time and inclination. After all, someone has to teach them that five dollars an hour may sound good, but doesn't go very far.

It's nice to see my children accepting responsibility, Lord. They've learned so much about life through their work: discipline, concern, commitment, how to budget their time and resources. Thank You for the opportunities that have come their way. Help them to get the most out of them, in all ways.

For thou shalt eat the labour of thine hands: happy shalt thou be, and it shall be well with thee.

Psalms 128:2

31 "What Do You Want to Be?"

When a child hits sixteen, his parents start thinking about his future with growing trepidation. Someone has to. A sixteen-year-old's only concern with the future revolves around his upcoming driver's license.

You have to start reminding him there's life after high school during his sophomore year of high school. Not that you want to nag him or force him into a career decision at this young age, but he does have to start facing reality pretty soon. He has to know that if college is not possible, a paying job is a certainty. If college is possible, he has to start looking at his choices, weeding out ways he's sure he doesn't want to make a living, and start recognizing his strengths.

The easiest way to approach this is usually through the process of elimination. First you mention the obvious choices: doctor, lawyer, engineer. The jobs that require lots of schooling and preparation. If he turns those down—and most children do as soon as they learn how many additional years of school are required before they begin earning something back—you try the next level while mentally adding up the tuition you've just been spared and trying not to look too happy.

This process rarely produces a decision on anything. It just gets his mind flowing in the right direction. The next step is to evaluate his strengths. Is there any one thing he excels at? *Anything* can help. If the only thing he's good at is pleasing girls, he may, after all, be a natural shoe salesman. Our older son spent his high school years building models and drawing machinery instead of studying his history. We thought he was wasting his time playing, when there were far more serious things he should be concentrating on. He's now studying to be an industrial designer—a person who gets paid for building models and drawing machinery. I never knew there was such a job, but he discovered what he could do and found a job to fit his talents and interests.

Our daughter has a talent for working with people and handling money, so she studied business and got a job doing both for a broker. I don't really understand what she does all day, but her father does, and he's happy, so I am, too.

We're now starting to work with our last child on this. He's a good writer, has a great imagination, and knows computers. I don't have any idea what he'll end up doing—writing computer programs, maybe—but he'll figure it out in the next few years.

The hardest part of this whole thing is the lack of resources available to parents and teens on careers. At the rate the world is changing, there are jobs out there that didn't exist twenty (or even two) years ago. Library books on this are all at least fifteen years old and useless. You just have to hope your son's high school or college guidance office has materials available and a counselor who has taken the time to look at them.

But don't count on the guidance office for much guidance. As well meaning and dedicated as those poor souls are, every one of them is overworked and underbudgeted. Just keeping schedules straight, dealing with disciplinary matters, and filling out college application requests is more than they can be expected to handle.

For the most part, you and your child are going to have to do your own legwork. But it's worth it. There's nothing more rewarding than seeing your child find what he's looking for and start out in life with a job he really loves.

Father, teach me to tread lightly here. My job's not to push my child into a job I like, but to encourage him to find one he likes. Help me show him his talents, find how they fit into the working world, and be a constant source of support as he searches for his own future.

Yet now be strong . . . and work: for I am with you, saith the Lord of hosts.

Haggai 2:4

32 Customizing

Steve doesn't know much about cars, yet; he's still mastering the art of moped riding without contusions. But he's planning ahead to the day he can afford to buy his first car and begin fixing it up.

He already has his older brother's promise of help and has picked up some information through watching Jim do and undo various parts, change oil, and all that good stuff boys do to their first cars. But Steve has always been conscious of how much he doesn't know about things, unlike some teens who barrel ahead and find out too late they're missing a vital piece of information. He worries in advance, arms himself with facts, practices in solitude, *then* goes and does things pretty well the first time.

So I wasn't too surprised when he asked how auto mechanics "learn that stuff" the other day. I told him some picked it up on the job, some went to school, and there were books on it. That seemed to satisfy him.

Now, I don't know a spark plug from a firefly, but I do know about books and about my son, so when I stopped at the bookstore today to pick up a novel for vacation reading, I picked him up a copy of Chilton's guide to auto repair. All 500-plus pages of it, at $21.95. I figured Bill and Jim would also make use of it, which made it an acceptable price.

Steve came home, leafed through it with a few awed "Wow"s, grinning ear to ear, then gave me a big hug before lugging it up to his room. He'll spend the next year studying that book, copying the illustrations, storing up its facts, and when he does get his first car, he'll know pretty well how to take it apart and put it back together.

Like I said, I don't know beans about cars. That didn't preclude me from helping Steve learn about them, though. Sometimes knowing where to find help is all that's required of a parent. And you get wonderful hugs as payment. It was worth the $21.95.

Lord, they want to know about more complex things as they grow older—things I don't understand at all. When there's something I can do to help them, show it to me, whether it's a book, an expert's name, or some long-forgotten fact I once knew.

As they grow older, our being able to help them in these ways will become one of the most important bonds between us.

And God said to Solomon, Because this was in thine heart, and thou hast not asked riches, wealth, or honour, nor the life of thine enemies, neither yet hast asked long life; but hast asked wisdom and knowledge for thyself . . . Wisdom and knowledge is granted unto thee. . . .

2 Chronicles 1:11, 12

33

Digitized

Can you look at a digital clock and really *know* what time it is? I can't. To me, "7:27" means nothing, while "Almost 7:30" means someone is going to be late for school. I have to look at a digital clock and translate what I see into *real* time.

My kids don't. They live in a digital world and can tell time either way. It strikes me that their brains must be radically different from mine to do this. I find that frightening. For one thing, it means every minute of their lives has its own meaning, while I live my life in fifteen-minute or half-hour segments. Sometimes I feel I'm missing valuable minutes from my day. On the other hand, I spend considerably less time looking at my wrist than they do, so I recapture a lot of minutes from that.

My children wear computers on their wrists which beep every hour on the hour to remind them how fast their day is going by. I wear a watch with absolutely no numbers on it. Sometimes I have trouble telling 8:00 A.M. from 9:00 A.M., but it doesn't really bother me. It would drive them crazy.

I tried wearing a digital watch one day. It gave me an anxiety attack. I found myself preoccupied with those dancing numbers, uncomfortable with all the little buttons that protruded from the watch's side. If I pushed the wrong one by accident, my watch would start counting off the seconds and some smug child would have to reset it for me.

I once put a digital alarm clock beside my bed because it was compact and cute and visible at 2:00 A.M. I never had to reach over and turn off the alarm—I was awake most of the night, watching the minutes flip down one at a time with a resounding "thunk."

There's a basic philosophical difference between children and adults involved here. They *enjoy* seeing time go by, while I want to hoard each minute. They spend a lot of their lives waiting for things to happen, like parties, graduations, dates, and driver's licenses. I'm in no rush to see any of those things happen.

But it gives you food for thought. After years of teaching them "When the big hand's on the twelve," you're suddenly living with a teenager who tells you, "But it's only twelve-seventeen. I'm not that late."

"You're twenty minutes late."

"Uh-uh. Seventeen. What's seventeen minutes?"

Nothing, to him. To me, it's almost half an hour! There's something different about his brain, and it bothers me.

We spend so much time waiting for things to happen, Lord. "When I get that promotion," we say, neglecting to treasure the days between now and then. Teach us to appreciate each day You give us to the fullest. Don't allow us to waste our years in waiting for "better times" when we should be busy building those times each day we live.

And he shall be like a tree planted by the rivers of water, that bringeth forth his fruit in his season; his leaf also shall not wither; and whatsoever he doeth shall prosper.

Psalms 1:3

34 Traditions

Traditions are a family's glue, vital and necessary, but watch out what you start. Little touches that seem cute when the kids are young will come back to haunt you for the next twenty-one years.

The first year we had a rug rat in the family, we bought two packages of plastic Christmas-tree ornaments for the low branches, thinking it would be nice if our firstborn survived the holidays. They were ugly, but safe. By the time Laura had learned that Christmas-tree ornaments are breakable and uneatable, we had another crawler, then a third.

Finally we deemed it safe to hang real ornaments down near floor level. We planned to leave the ugly plastic ones in their boxes and install lovely new breakable ones on the tree. But by then, Laura was nine, Jim was six, and no power on earth was going to keep *their* ornaments off the tree! Tradition.

To overcome one tradition, start another. If the kids wanted their own ornaments, so be it; I took them out and let each pick out a new ornament of their very own. After two or three years of this, they allowed us to retire the plastic ornaments with fitting honor. Now each child has his own collection of decorations that matches his taste and brings forth cries of recognition as the ornament box is unloaded each year. Soon we'll need three trees to hold them all. Worse yet, I know the day is coming when they move out and set up their own trees, each taking along his collection of ornaments and leaving us with nothing to hang except those ugly plastic bulbs!

Traditions do ebb and flow, changing slightly as children grow. We started putting the Christmas stockings on the kids' beds to give ourselves a few more minutes' sleep when they were toddlers. They loved it, all of them gathering on one bed at 5:00 A.M. to compare stockings, then coming in to wake us up.

Soon we found ourselves staying up later and later on Christmas Eve to do stocking duty (and bring out the unwrapped Santa presents). In no time at all, they were going to bed hours after we were. Santa had to get up at 4:00 A.M. to be sure they were all asleep when he delivered the stockings. Santa didn't like that!

Now our daughter buys the stocking stuffers, driving off with our money on Christmas Eve to find a store that's still open. She does it much better than I do, and enjoys herself—it's a tradition.

We have one Christmas tradition that I truly love. After years of waking early to care for youngsters, I can no longer sleep late, especially on Christmas. After Santa makes his rounds at four or five in the morning, I'm awake for the day. I sneak downstairs, plug in the tree, and enjoy its glow in the predawn darkness. Remembering to turn up the heat, I make a pot of coffee, set out breakfast, and then, at 6:00 A.M., joyfully turn on the Christmas carols and go wake up the whole house!

Oh, they grumble about it—loudly—but every year I

hear one of them say to a friend, "We'll be up at six. My mother wakes up the whole house then—every year!" Hey, it's a tradition!

Make me aware of the fact that what I do will be remembered by my children, Lord. They remember more than little rituals and traditions. They remember how I speak about other people, how I act in times of happiness or crisis, what I believe in and hold to be right. Let my daily life teach them to walk uprightly all their days.

And ye shall teach them your children, speaking of them when thou sittest in thine house, and when thou walkest by the way, when thou liest down, and when thou risest up.

Deuteronomy 11:19

35

Closets

Every fall, as soon as the kids leave for college or begin classes wherever they are, I'm gripped by an overwhelming compulsion. I pace the suddenly silent house, trying in vain to control myself. Soon I trudge upstairs, a box of garbage bags tucked purposefully under my arm. It's closet-cleaning time!

The kids know this is going to happen. They put off leaving me alone with their closets as long as possible.

They open the closet doors and look longingly at a year's accumulation of torn posters, outworn jeans, unworn dress shirts, broken models, shoes without laces. They catalog the tiny fragments of paper scattered amid the sleeping bags and comforters. They put orphaned stuffed animals up on the closet shelf, hoping my compulsion won't be strong enough to include climbing on a chair (it's rarely *that* strong). They throw me baleful looks. But eventually they do leave.

And I go to work. First comes the clothing shuffle: transferring outgrown or unloved clothing from an older child's closet to that of a younger child. There are obvious limitations to be observed here if you have a mixed bag of children; I've never found a way to convince a boy that girls' jeans are the same as boys'. Fifty percent of the carefully transferred clothing will immediately be recognized as hand-me-downs and never worn. Another 25 percent won't fit or be judged worthy of wearing. But the 25 percent that's accepted is pure bonus, saving you a small fortune now that jeans cost over twenty dollars a pair. Tastes varying between children as they do, that shirt you bought your older son for Christmas may actually be worn before the coming holidays. It's chancy, but sometimes you get lucky.

Then I arrange all the remaining clothes: pants in the center, real shirts next, sweaters, sports jacket, then sweatshirts and jeans. There's parental logic to this arrangement. Since kids will always grab what's in the center of the closet, that's where I put the clothes I'd like to see them wear. Everything they like gets hidden at the ends of the pipe. This tactic never works, but I keep trying.

I look at the shelf, but rarely touch it. I don't like being hit on the head by game and puzzle boxes, and if I so much as touched that precariously balanced pile, I'd get brained, so I generally leave it as it is. It gives them a safe place to put their really treasured possessions, too.

Closet floors are fair game, though. This is where a good supply of garbage bags—the big ones you use for the grass clippings—is essential. Some really good, caring mothers will actually sit down on the floor and sort through the junk. They also look forward to root canal work. I pick out the obviously valuable stuff, then use a shovel on everything else lying down there. It never pays to look too closely at anything on a closet floor. It may move.

That should be the end of it, but it seldom is. In order to put away the salvageable items from the closet floor, I have to find space in a drawer or on a shelf or under a bed. This requires rearranging, which escalates into another garbage-bag binge. Soon I've progressed to the desk, which they will presumably need to use in the near future for homework, but which is now piled high with old magazines, tiny model pieces, broken pencils, forgotten phone numbers, a year's worth of dust, and $1.33 in pennies.

If I'm lucky, the garbageman will come before the victim returns from college, but they don't keep high school students that long, so I try to bury the bags under bags of *real* garbage. I've had kids out there digging through the garbage with flashlights in their mouths and murder in their hearts.

Do I feel guilty about all this? Not really. If they'd do their own weeding out, I'd be more than happy to stop, but a closet whose doors will no longer shut is going to get cleaned out by somebody—and soon. As long as it has to be me, I'll continue to swear everything usable is still there, if they can find where it's now stored. But the truth is, kids, I lied. I threw out a *lot!*

Deciding what to keep and what to throw away is always hard, whether we're talking about clothes, memories, or attitudes. In all of these, and the countless other daily decisions I have to make, I look to You for guidance, Lord. Give me the discretion I need to make the right choices.

. . . keep sound wisdom and discretion: So shall they be life unto thy soul, and grace to thy neck. Then shalt thou walk in thy way safely, and thy foot shall not stumble.

Proverbs 3:21–23

36 Seventeen

In our state, it's tempting to go down to the nearest Motor Vehicle office and walk in singing "Happy Birthday," since most of the people in line will be celebrating their seventeenth birthday by skipping school and taking their road test. It's a rite of passage that even the schools seem to honor.

It also marks a radical change of life for your family. Once your child gets a driver's license, childhood is over and young adulthood has begun. You can fight its physical manifestations by withholding car keys and imposing curfews, but it's really a mental change that you can't control. A seventeen-year-old with a license is so much *older* than a sixteen-year-old.

Suddenly he'll become responsible and eager to run to the store in a blizzard to pick up milk for your coffee. He'll drive his little brother to the Hobby Shop to buy models. He'll even take the dog to the vet. It's wonderful. It lasts only until he saves up enough money to buy a rusted-out Camero.

If your son is slightly older than his friends, he'll begin running a free taxi service. You'll get strange calls at 11:00 P.M.: "Tell Jim I'm at Joe's and *desperate!*" Of course you haven't seen Jim since dinner and expect to be asleep when he returns, but you dutifully tack the message to the banister and go to bed wondering exactly who's desperate and for what.

Now it's quite possible that my family is not a normal family, so take this with caution, but our daughter is an excellent driver. We've never worried one hour about her since she got her license (I'm probably stretching the truth a bit, but it's all relative).

We started out with the same confidence in our son, until one day I overheard a friend call him Crash. Sure we knew about his fender benders (three in three months—we were so *naive!*). But one was not his fault, the second was mutual, and the third was all his. Still, when another seventeen-year-old calls your son Crash, you develop an instant, overwhelming unease! Looking back, you realize he's put every car you own into the body shop in a very short time. The little man who owns the shop now waves as you drive by, a big smile on his face.

Check around, though. Chances are, his friends haven't done any better, and some have done far worse. It's nothing short of a miracle when all of them manage to survive their first year of driving without spending some time in the hospital. The sad part is that not all of them do.

I don't know when it ends, not having lived that long yet. I do know that the car he bought with his own money has fared far better than those he borrowed from us. It's been a long time since the last ticket, which is a good sign, but not anything I'm ready to count on. So although I used to wave my daughter off cheerfully on her three-hour drive to college, I still make him call me when he gets in after his one-hour drive. I love you, Jim—I just wish you were driving a horse instead of a T-Bird!

I know Your eye is on the sparrow, Lord, and my children are as loved by You as they are by me, but I still get frightened for them. Help me trust them as they mature—keep them safe until then!

. . . The beloved of the Lord shall dwell in safety by him; and the Lord shall cover him all the day long, and he shall dwell between his shoulders.

Deuteronomy 33:12

37   Rage

Nothing in the world inspires rage like a teenager. Cruelty to animals, injustice, discrimination—these can all make me furious—but they pale before the pure white rage a teenager can ignite in me.

We have to distinguish between anger and rage, here. I'm angry when my son exceeds his curfew and I hear him come in at 2:00 A.M. But when I wake up and his car is not in the driveway at 6:00 A.M., I fly into a rage. I'm angry when he gets a speeding ticket; when he gets one while driving his little brother, I'm in a rage.

See the difference? Any adult can; no teenager can. Rage is the product of fear, pure and simple. As such, it varies from parent to parent. Quite often, it varies within a parent, depending on her mood or how dinner's sitting with her. There's no telling what will produce anger and what will frighten you enough to cause rage. And if this is confusing to a teenager, it's no clearer to the parent. It just *is*, and you have to live with it.

Some parents with limited imaginations and saintly children probably never know rage. I happen to have an unlimited imagination and normal children, so I know it well.

Okay, let's define the emotional and physical aspects of anger and rage. When I'm angry, I usually yell. My face turns red, my glasses slip down my nose, and I begin to hyperventilate. I threaten, I bully, I pout, I punish. It's loud and unpleasant, but as soon as I get it out of my system, it's over and we can be friends.

Rage is a purer emotion. In a rage, I can't see anything. I might even mistake the five-foot-eleven-inch son for the five-foot-ten-inch one, which can be dangerous and unfair. In a rage, my face is dead white and cold. My fingers are numb. I'm not hyperventilating—I'm barely breathing. I don't yell, because there is no connection between my brain and my tongue. I am truly beyond words.

I'm downright dangerous, is what I am! If a teenager scares me enough to produce a rage, he's in more physical danger from me than he was from whatever caused the rage. Being speechless, I'm likely to get his attention by throwing a book at him. Luckily, I can't see well in a rage, so I usually miss. Once I have his attention, I start swatting wildly in his direction. When he holds me off with his long arms and laughs at me, I kick him in the shins until someone rescues him. All in all, I behave exactly like a two-year-old in the midst of a full-blown temper tantrum. Later, when I've cooled down to plain old angry and the child dares to come into the same room with me, I do my yelling and explaining. And I apologize.

I don't get into rages very often—maybe once a year— but when I do, it makes an impression. I've never had to rage on the same subject twice. I don't like myself when I act like that; it scares me. Luckily, it also scares them. They're learning the parameters of my rage, which means they're scaring me less often, which means they're living safer lives, which is undoubtedly a good thing.

Father, keep me from rage, whether You do it by controlling me or by controlling my children. Let us work things out through love and reason and not cause fear in one another by irresponsible actions and reactions.

Cease from anger, and forsake wrath. . . .

Psalms 37:8

38 Buck Fever

Sometimes you feel terrible about sticking to your guns.

The men in our family hunt, mostly for pheasant, and our boys were brought up learning firearm safety, how to hunt over a dog, how to kill no more than we'd eat. The three of them only go out two or three times a year, but they do it well when they go, and it's brought them all closer while teaching the boys skills that are becoming uncommon today.

Our older son took to it with the most enthusiasm, becoming a remarkable shot for his age and experience.

He was good, and he was responsible. I never worried about anyone's safety when Jim was out there.

But I said no when he asked to go deer hunting. He'd never been before, his father wasn't going, and so many more accidents take place during deer season. It wasn't that I thought he was dangerous—it was everyone else I mistrusted.

Bill backed me up, admitting to the same qualms I'd voiced. Maybe next year. So the group went without Jim, and his best friend used the stand Jim had built for himself. Twenty minutes after climbing up onto that stand, he got an eight-point buck. Jim's buck.

Jim was mad—at me, at his father, at the stupid buck that should have been in our freezer. And, of course, there were no accidents that day.

I felt like dog food. I hadn't trusted my son to do what I knew he could do well. He would have gotten that buck—no doubt about that—and I love venison! I chewed myself out about it for days. Then I realized something: Even if I'd known the day's results in advance, I still wouldn't have let him go. I'd made the right decision and stuck to it, and even though I'd been proven wrong, the decision was still right.

Fall's coming again soon, and I expect the question is coming again, too. It's two years later, now, and this time I'll probably let him go, and he'll probably come back with nothing. But two years ago, I was right. It's not always easy, sticking to your guns.

Father, I hate to say no sometimes. And often I'm too cautious or proven wrong. But that's my job, so I'll just do it the best I can and have confidence that You'll help me to know when I need to say no.

I rejoice therefore that I have confidence in you in all things.

2 Corinthians 7:16

39   Jocks and Grinds

I've never had a child who was a jock, but then I've never had a grind, either. All things considered, I'm glad my kids fell into that anonymous mass of the unlabeled—except when they were applying to colleges.

Not that they didn't have athletic and intellectual abilities. My daughter holds the high school record for getting hit in the shins the most during one field hockey season (she never limped back for a second season). On the academic side, she made it through a good college with great grades and still had time for a little fun.

My older son was never well coordinated, but his intramural floor hockey team was noted for being the fastest, roughest bunch of barbarians on the floor. They had determination enough to make up for any lack of athletic talent. Academically, he got through two years of Spanish without being strung up by his teacher and surprised everyone by turning into a talented draftsman.

My younger son is showing signs of aspiring to jockdom, but he isn't there yet. He wrestles moderately well and works as a lifeguard, but has no interest in football, basketball, or any of those other good sports they give scholarships for. Academically, he holds the school record for teachers' notes that begin, "Steven is not working up to his potential." If he ever did work up to his potential, he'd scare us all to death.

Their normality is okay by me. Jocks lead a hard life. They have no time to themselves, are constantly putting their bodies in jeopardy, and work twice as hard as everyone else to handle all the demands on them. The *real* jocks—the ones who do it all well—deserve all the attention they earn, and their parents pay for all their scholarships with years of carpooling and physical therapy sessions. If being a jock has a few extra benefits (girls!), that's okay, too.

On the other side of the coin, I also admire grinds. Someone has to. There's something to be said for a kid who has the courage to be noticeably unpopular, to carry pens in little plastic pocket protectors, to talk openly in the halls of quantum mechanics, and to admire the lines on an IBM mainframe. A true grind has every bit as much guts as a football lineman. And you can bet that the man or woman who finally develops an immunization shot for cancer will have gone through school as a grind.

But most students are neither jock nor grind. Most fall somewhere in the middle, having their share of talents and their individual lack of abilities—just like their parents. Personally, I always prayed none of my kids would turn into geniuses or develop extraordinary talents. I wouldn't know what to do with them, this particular problem not being common in my family. I suppose I would have adjusted and coped with it, but I'm just as happy I didn't have to. Still, I wish a few colleges would award scholarships to students who plug along, show determination in their lives, and graduate from high school with parents who still admit to loving and admiring them!

Father, it's not easy for a parent to admit to himself that his child is just a normal, good kid; not in this age of geniuses. But You arranged it so this world is supported, protected, and perpetuated by people who are in the main not geniuses—just normal, good kids grown up into decent, loving adults. Help me realize that when I have the urge to push my child too hard in the wrong direction. Let me find pleasure in his special abilities and not look too closely at his unavoidable faults, for You know his worth far better than I.

I have no greater joy than to hear that my children walk in truth.

3 John 4

40 Save It

I am no longer allowed to throw out ratty replaced furniture. The plastic-topped kitchen table with its scratched surface and matching set of chairs with their punctured rattan backs and slashed foam-filled seats—they're in the cellar. The gold wingback easy chair that the dog and cat slept on for years and that clashes with the new red rugs—that's down there.

There's a lot of junk in our cellar. A Ping-Pong table that has been used as a model-building table, for example. Its green surface is now multicolored from years of misdirected spray paint; newspaper is welded to its surface with model glue. The net, paddles, and balls disappeared years ago, but the table remains. There's an end table that I started to refinish ten years ago, made a mess of, and abandoned. There's a lovely wooden playpen with no cushion. The frame and headboard to a queen-size bed hold up one cellar wall; two twin mattresses and box springs are stored away somewhere.

The truth is, you could furnish an apartment with all the junk we have down there. That's precisely the reason I can't throw it away; I have two children who have designs on my junk! Every time I threaten to toss something, I hear squeals of, "No! I'll take it when I get my own place."

I'm sure they will, too. Not to mention the good stuff that will be carried out my front door. My camera went to college with my son last weekend. It'll never return to my possession again. My daughter has a table service for six squirreled away in her closet, in case she decides to give a dinner party in her room some evening. My husband's tools are disappearing one at a time.

I don't really mind. I'm better off than they are at this point and will gladly supply whatever I can when they need it. But if they'd let me, I'd prefer to buy them a new kitchen table when they move out. I can just hear their new next-door neighbors now: "*This* came from your parents'?"

There's nothing really wrong with any of the used furniture my children plan to take from me, Lord. Thank You for making them practical and frugal. Help me overcome the feelings of embarrassment I'm harboring about this and realize that what's junk to me may be a treasured memory to my children.

Silver and gold have I none; but such as I have give I thee. . . .

Acts 3:6

41

SATs

I wish I could think of more accurate and descriptive words for those initials than *Scholastic Aptitude Testing*, but if I did, they'd probably be unprintable. Not that I have anything against the firm that runs them or the colleges that use them; it's just such an inhumane process.

Far too much depends on this test. Unless your child is in the genius class, the pressure is too much—for you, not necessarily for your child. I raised my kids saying, "Just do your best. That's all we ask," and it worked out okay. They all led well-balanced lives and got their share of As and Ds. Then they took their PSATs in their junior years and I turned into a monster.

To a junior, college testing is a yuk. They don't even know what they're doing Saturday night, so why worry about something that's a year away? As a result, they do lousy on the test. No matter how you figure it out—by percentiles, stanines, or neighborhood comparison—your child is not college material.

I suppose there are parents whose kids do well, but there are far more who spend the next year in a state of near panic. They yell things like, "This is your *future* we're talking about. Get serious!" They spend $500 for a foolproof SAT course guaranteed to raise a score one hundred points (big deal—one hundred points brings him up to subnormal). They buy computer programs and books that no student ever looks at. Above all, they worry.

After a year of this, any kid catches on and goes into the real test a nervous wreck. As soon as you see that stunned look on his face after the test, you go through the process of signing him up for another shot at it, plus Achievement tests the following month.

Did you ever fill out one of those application forms? First of all, you have to find the little lost card that has his Social Security number on it, since that's the true identifier of your child. Everything gets written in little boxes, but you also have to color in little circles underneath each letter or number (with a number 2 pencil. Erase any mistakes totally, or your son may be classified as a female. Wear your reading glasses). It takes a good hour to do it right, and even then, you're not sure. But if your kid's a genius, you only have to do it three times; maybe you can even trust him to do it himself.

Eventually your child will come out with an acceptable score or you'll all give up and take what you get. And what's been gained by all this agony? Your child, who was always a little underconfident, now knows for a fact that he's "inferior" because he didn't get the magic number of 1200. He's not going to M.I.T. or Harvard. Not that he wanted to, but that doesn't matter. The choice has been taken away from him, and that's what matters. This is when a kid learns he really can't fly.

Hey, it's not all bad. A high school senior needs to know that life has its disappointments and that he has to have realistic goals. I think a lot of kids are relieved to get mediocre marks and be able to go to a mediocre college where they can have a little fun with their mediocre friends. But I do think it's a lesson that should be learned within the family, not from an impersonal testing service.

It's not easy to see a child learn about reality the hard way, Lord. I want to protect him a little longer. But it's time to let go; we both know that. So he's going to get hurt by a basically uncaring world, and there's nothing I can or should do about it, except reassure him of my love, and Yours. I pray that's enough to ease his pain.

He shall not be afraid of evil tidings: his heart is fixed, trusting in the Lord.

Psalms 112:7

42 College Interviews

It's a crisp fall weekend, and the ivy is calling—time to go visit some colleges with your senior. This takes more planning than you realize.

College catalogs have been pouring in all summer. Some you've sent for, some just arrived on their own.

Your child hasn't looked at any of them, and won't until forced to. *Hint:* Most of the ones you sent for won't accept your child; all the unsolicited ones will. There's a two-sided warning in there that parents should listen to, but won't.

The first thing to do is check under "Application Process" in a college catalog and try to decipher what a given college really wants. Some honestly don't want to talk to applicants. You take a group tour and go home. Do this at just one college. All group tours are the same. All dorm rooms are the same. It's a waste of time. If your child absolutely, positively wants to go to one of these colleges, it's worth a visit *after* he's been accepted.

Other colleges insist on face-to-face interviews with prospective students, their parents, and the parents' current income-tax return. Your chances are pretty slim here. First of all, you won't be able to get your son into a suit and tie or your daughter into a dress. Even if the Admissions Office is filled with kids in jeans, your son still needs the suit and tie. Those kids in jeans are either potential all-American jocks or math wizards.

Most colleges give you a little leeway. You can come for an interview and tour or just the tour. What you decide on depends on how much you or your child wants that college. *Note:* There's no guarantee you and your child will agree on this evaluation. Compromise. If anybody's serious about it, go for the interview. Tell your child to speak in complete sentences, smile when appropriate, and avoid any mention of his love for Heavy Metal.

At all college visits, be sure you learn a few vital facts. Ask what percentage of the sophomore class doesn't get a room on campus. If it's over 10 percent, are you ready to have your child living in an off-campus apartment? In a college town? Ask the name of the food service the college uses, then go home and talk to some college freshmen and decide if your child can live on pizza for four years. Ask what percentage of incoming freshmen actually graduate from that school and how many bug out after one year. Ask if freshmen are allowed to bring cars (your son or daughter will think of that one), then check out the parking and traffic situation on your tour.

Most important, look at the students around you. Are they boisterous and happy, or do they slog around with serious faces? How many obviously spaced-out students can you count in front of one building? How many well-fed stray dogs do you spot? A college without friendly stray dogs has no heart, and I wouldn't send my kids there.

We've been through this twice and still have one more child to go. It's not anyone's idea of fun, but the better the job you do of it now, the less the chances are that you'll have to redo it in one year when your child decides to transfer to a new college!

I'm not ready to make this decision, Lord. How can I tell what a college is really like in one short visit? There are so many choices, so many variables. Guide us through these few months. Help us to know the colleges that are fitting; warn us about those that aren't.

I will instruct thee and teach thee in the way which thou shalt go: I will guide thee with mine eye.

Psalms 32:8

43 Application Forms

College application forms are a marvelous little world of their own, bearing absolutely no relationship to reality. Generally, the longer and more involved they are, the less chance your child has of being accepted, a high school senior's attention span being what it is—short!

Only parents take application forms seriously. No child knows his own Social Security number, what summer job he had as a freshman, or if he played three or four years' worth of floor hockey. Only parents know that stuff. Since these forms should be typed to make a good impression, go ahead and fill in this part yourself, throwing in a minor misspelling or two so the admissions committee will think your son can type.

Some colleges want to know more than name, address, and SAT I.D. number. "What made you decide to apply to

Horatio State College?" for example. *Note:* "My mother" is not a wise answer, even if it's true. If you think it's a good idea that your son answer these questions himself (and it is), don't just hand him a pen and leave the room. Talk through his answers, make him write them down on scrap paper, then edit before typing. You only get one shot, so make it a good one.

If your child has any talent whatsoever that can be demonstrated or documented, send it along. Drawings, tapes of recitals, creative writing, certificates of perfect Sunday school attendance—anything that will make his application stand out from the 10,021 other applications for the 2,010 freshman openings.

Many colleges also require teacher recommendations. This is tricky. Do you ask the teacher who gave your son an $A-$ in health? How about the $B+$ in history, who wouldn't know your son if he tripped over him? Or there's the $C+$ in algebra II, who really knew and liked your son but couldn't justify a B for him. My gut feeling was to go with the $C+$ teacher, but none of my kids ever got into an Ivy League school, so maybe the $A-$ in health is the correct answer. Whoever you choose, mail those forms to him early, before he gets swamped. *Don't* enclose a ten-dollar check for "postage"!

The one you really have to watch out for is the peer recommendation, where your son's best friend writes a letter about him. A college can tell a lot about your child from this, especially if he runs around with a bunch of illiterates! Of course he can always butter up the preppy president of the student council for a week and then ask him to do the honors. Some smart kid is going to make a fortune writing these things, if more colleges start using them.

Then comes the final agony: the application essay. Not all colleges require them; engineers aren't expected to write coherent paragraphs, for example. But if your kid's going for the big leagues (Ivy, Big Ten), he'll have to do one. You wouldn't believe the lengths some kids go to on these, to appear intelligent and stand out from the crowd. It was all I could do to get my kids to write something (*anything*) the proper length on the proper subject. It took weeks of hounding to produce two hundred and fifty words of sheer drivel. But drivel is better than nothing, so I fixed the spelling and typed it out.

Now you have it all together. The transcript request has gone to the guidance counselor; you've requested SAT scores to be sent to the college; the peer recommendation's with the student council president; the teacher recommendation is sitting at the bottom of someone's briefcase. The form's complete, the essay's done. Write out a $35 check and mail the sucker off.

That's one. Only seven more to go!

Lord, this is a complex, frustrating, expensive procedure. Help us out, here. Give me patience. Give my child a little ambition and perseverance. Show us the way through this maze and get him into the college that You know will meet his needs.

But continue thou in the things which thou hast learned and hast been assured of, knowing of whom thou hast learned them; And that from a child thou hast known the holy scriptures, which are able to make thee wise unto salvation through faith which is in Christ Jesus.

2 Timothy 3:14, 15

44 Acceptance and Rejection

It's April of your child's senior year, and you're both suffering from Senioritis. For the next month, the most important man in your life is the mailman—the one who brings the thick or thin letters from colleges.

It used to be good news came in thick envelopes and bad in thin, but colleges are getting sneaky, and some thin ones are good now. They all came addressed to my children—I opened them. Who could wait?

You win some, you lose some, but the first rejection always hurts. The kids take it fairly well, while I fume, "What do you mean, my child's not good enough for you? See if I ever apply to *you* again!" This is personal! This is an institutional attack on my parenting skills and my eighteen-year investment of time, energy, and tutoring.

The kids do better. "It was too far away, anyway." (Or too big, too small, too snobbish, too rural, too urban.)

Eventually it comes down to choosing among those that want your child. The colleges get three months to make their decision; you get two weeks, tops. There are a thousand ways to sort colleges, and no rational way to make a decision. Leave it to the kid—he has to live there. At this point, your job's downgraded to signing the checks for tuition deposit, room deposit, parents' activity fee (huh?), security deposit, insurance fee, and meal plan deposit.

Somewhere along the way, your child will fill out a questionnaire to help the college assign roommates. You'll learn a lot about your kid by looking over his shoulder.

"A coed dorm? You want a *coed* dorm?" This is usually addressed to a daughter.

"You want a roommate who goes to bed early and studies without music? Since when? Don't lie on this— they've already accepted you."

"The book says Berry Hall is a party dorm. Why not choose Smith? Berry, huh?"

"What's the difference between coed by floor and coed by suite? You're *kidding!*"

Finally all the forms are filled in, the checks written. It's over. Come September, your child is going off to a college you only vaguely remember, in a city that looked vaguely dangerous, with a bunch of other freshmen who will vaguely resemble your child. To live with a roommate (hopefully of the same sex) who loves to party during the week, sleep late, and study with music. They should get along just fine!

Okay, Lord, I give up. I'm not making these decisions, even if I do have some definite opinions, here. All I'm doing is pointing out the pros and cons and then trusting You to help him make the right choices. He's mature enough to know what he wants; You're faithful to provide any guidance he needs. It's not my decision to make anymore.

Trust in the Lord with all thine heart; and lean not unto thine own understanding. In all thy ways acknowledge him, and he shall direct thy paths.

Proverbs 3:5, 6

45

Graduation

It takes two weeks to graduate from high school: fourteen days of uninterrupted partying, punctuated by a one-hour ceremony no one but a parent really wants to attend. Seniors love the idea of graduating until it involves wearing real shoes and walking fifty feet to collect their diplomas, and the only thing that will make a senior attend a family graduation party is the possibility of high-class gifts.

It's a stressful two weeks for parents who can't quite

remember their own high school graduation. Those who do remember tend to moan a lot.

One day you'll see your child for the ten minutes it takes him to come downstairs, eat cold pizza for breakfast, and place a few phone calls. The next day you'll have fifteen seniors camping out in your kitchen, eating like locusts. There will be no set schedule to count on. You may receive a late-night call from your scholar saying, "I'm at the Shore. I'll be back in time for tomorrow's party." On the other hand, one morning you may stumble over the snoring form of a classmate who never made it home. (Yes, you do have to call his parents, even if it's only 8:00 A.M.) It's a no-holds-barred two weeks.

Once you resign yourself, it can be fun for you, too. Just insist on basic safety at this point and enjoy the little animals. Feed anything that opens its mouth or your refrigerator. Loan money to the broke (as long as you've known the individual for longer than ten minutes). Drive home those who shouldn't have driven to your house in the first place. Keep in touch with other perplexed and worried parents. Above all—*be there*.

I'd about had it one day until I heard a sad young voice from my kitchen. "This is the last weekend we'll all be together, guys."

He was immediately corrected. "No, it's not. We've got all summer."

"But we'll all be working. Then you guys go off to college. This is our last weekend all together."

He was right. I went in and cooked them two pounds of spaghetti. There wasn't much else I could do for them, was there?

*About all I can do now is be here, Lord. I hope it's enough.
They're all going through such an emotional, heady time now,
feeling so young and strong and brave and frightened—all at
once. May they truly enjoy these times and use their freedom
wisely.*

For ye shall go out with joy, and be led forth with peace:
the mountains and the hills shall break forth before you
into singing, and all the trees of the field shall clap their
hands.

Isaiah 55:12

46   Conversations

There are some conversations parents don't want to
hear. Whether your teen is locked into the hall closet with
the telephone or standing out under your streetlight on a
summer's night, you just don't want to know any more
than you already overheard.

Here are some little snippets that can drive you
wild:

"Joe's parents will be away. I'll bring the chips, you bring the. . . ."

"The drive-in movie was so dull, we. . . ."

"I would have failed that exam, if it wasn't for. . . ."

"Mary Ann? You know, the girl who. . . ."

"Of course, I love you! What do I have to do. . . ."

"I've got five dollars. You've got ten. Let's go out and. . . ."

"Let's take our little brothers and. . . .'

"I'm going to paint. . . ."

"Then the principal said to me. . . ."

"You think that's bad? The state trooper told me. . . ."

"My parents are asleep. Let's. . . ."

On second thought, maybe it's time to stick your head out the window and tell him it's past his curfew!

Father, I know sometimes I read more into the things I overhear than is really there. But other times, I know I'm hearing right.

Give me discernment about this; teach me what not to hear and what I should really listen to.

Lo this, we have searched it, so it is; hear it, and know thou it for thy good.

Job 5:27

47

Axioms:
Eighteen to Twenty-one

All college freshmen solve the problems of the world before Thanksgiving and spend the vacation telling you how *your* generation messed up *their* world.

If college is less than three hours from home, Laundromats are optional.

No college student needs a telephone credit card; that's what they make quarters for.

If your son's not bringing home dirty laundry, he's found himself a girlfriend.

The trip to college in the fall can be made in one car; the trip from college in the spring requires two cars or a van.

Your child's roommate is telling his parents the same horror stories about your son that you're hearing about him.

The food at college is only half as bad as your son makes it out to be.

Sleep and food are optional, fun is essential.

All boys lose ten pounds during their first term of college; all girls gain twenty.

Colleges don't call you when your child is sick; you find out when Blue Cross refuses to pay for the emergency-room visit.

48

Laundry List

I used to be fairly certain about what I'd find when I washed the kids' clothes: towels (damp), crew sox (inside out), jeans (one leg inside out), assorted shirts (blue or red), and underwear (Sear's best). But now my kids are earning a little money and I'm finding surprises in there.

I used to find:

1. *Solid color towels*, the darker the better. Now I'm finding a full set of striped towels my son brought

home from college. Nice towels, better than I'd ever buy.

2. *Flannel pajamas*. There are no longer any pajamas in their hamper.

3. *White crew sox with colored stripes*. Now we have knee-high stockings, panty hose, pink crew sox, men's dress darks, and worn-out white crew sox with colored stripes.

4. *Sear's jockey shorts*. Someone bought himself Jockey jockey shorts, red bikini briefs, and one pair of boxer shorts with fraternity brothers' names written all over them (I didn't ask).

5. *Carter's little girls' briefs*. This change is too drastic and variable to be cataloged. Suffice it to say, they all look very uncomfortable and insubstantial, to me.

6. *White T-shirts with short sleeves*. We now have rib-knit athletic shirts, mainly in black, which are worn as real shirts all summer—in public.

7. *Knit polo shirts*. These have been replaced by rock-group T-shirts with the neckline and sleeves ripped off, OP T-shirts, or T-shirts advertising faraway resorts.

8. *Dress shirts*. Replaced by knit polo shirts (we're on a downward spiral, here).

9. *Jeans, blue*. Nothing replaces blue jeans.

10. *Slacks, dress*. These only appear after a forced dress-up day at school or a visit to Grandpa's.

11. *Skirts, washable*. All skirts are now dry-clean-only.

12. *Girls' shirts, washable*. *See* number 11.

Things are changing around here. At least I can count on the damp towels being there, mildewing away, when I open the hamper. A few things never change.

Change shows up everywhere when there are teens in the house. Help me to understand this is natural and good, Father, that even their changing clothing indicates they are maturing, thinking for themselves, becoming the individuals You designed them to be.

Of old hast thou laid the foundation of the earth: and the heavens are the work of thy hands. They shall perish, but thou shalt endure: yea, all of them shall wax old like a garment; as a vesture shalt thou change them, and they shall be changed: But thou art the same, and thy years shall have no end. The children of thy servants shall continue, and their seed shall be established before thee.

Psalms 102:25–28

49

The Shore

It's Friday evening, and I have the feeling I'm being conned out of at least twenty dollars. I'm not supposed to realize this, of course. Neither am I supposed to have any idea what's running through my son's mind as we carry out this ritual, but I'm an old hand at this, so I do.

* * *

"Okay if I go to the Shore tomorrow with the guys?"

"Who's driving?"

"Sam." *Five of us in the car, cruising down the Parkway with the windows down and the music up, my hair blowing in my eyes. Seeing how fast we can go through the tollbooths and still get the quarters in the baskets. Kerplunk . . . kerplunk . . . oops.*

"A day trip?"

"Yeah. We'll leave early and be back late." *Finding a place to park and unpacking the car. Radio, cooler, metallic sunglasses no one can see my eyes through. Sand in my sneakers, sun on my hair.*

"Are you taking dates?"

"No. Just the guys this time." *Looking for a good place on the beach. Row on row of bronzed girls, one of them smiling up at me as I scatter sand on her towel by accident. It was an accident, too. White teeth, blonde hair.*

"Isn't the water still too cold for swimming?"

"That's okay." *The sun burning my shoulders while we talk*

to the girls next to us. Digging my toes deep into the cool sand. Building a castle at the water's edge with the help of the friendly blonde. Big, complicated, impressive castle. She loves it.

"Is the boardwalk open this early?"

"Um-hum." *Rides and games and water slides. Winning the precise stuffed animal she wants on my fourteenth try. Expensive, but worth it for a hug of thanks.*

"You'll be back late?"

"We'll leave after dark." *The boardwalk for dinner. Anything you could possibly want to eat. She likes her hot dogs with chili, just like I do. Then a cone to eat down by the water. Walking away from the crowd, water up to our knees. A little splashing, just to tease. Trading phone numbers as the shoreline disappears into the night.*

"Need any money?"

"I could use a twenty." *Long ride home, trying not to hurt my burn, Pete's elbow in my ribs as he sleeps. Blonde hair, white teeth on my mind.*

"Have a good time."

"Thanks." *Freedom!*

I remember those days, Lord. I know how important they are for him and how he'll remember his days at the Shore forever.

Rejoice, O young man, in thy youth; and let thy heart cheer thee in the days of thy youth. . . .

Ecclesiastes 11:9

50 Hair

Somewhere between the ages of seventeen and twenty-one, I lost control of my son's hair. I know those are the ages that apply in our family because I can still get my seventeen-year-old to the barber's with a week's worth of grousing, but my twenty-one-year-old's hair is cascading below his shoulders.

Hair is not something worth breaking up a family over. I know this. I know that eventually his girlfriend or his employer will tell him, "Cut it, or else," and that will be that. I know someday I will see his eyes again; if I'm lucky, maybe even his ears. He has beautiful eyes and adorable ears.

We can get him to have it trimmed by telling him his grandfather's coming to town. However, his idea of a trim still leaves Grandpa shaking his head and convinced his grandson is a hippie, so even that's not worth the effort now.

Why does his hair infuriate me so? Probably because he's only kept it long since he found out how much it bugs me. It's his version of rebellion, his way of telling me to get lost without getting his shins kicked. I seriously doubt that he prefers it long, since he's a very conservative person at heart.

If I'm right, he can keep his long hair. It's a rebellion I can easily live with, compared to some of the alternatives.

It will still set my teeth on edge and cause me to sputter at him, but that's exactly the reaction he's hoping for.

Meanwhile, my seventeen-year-old's growing closer to the magical point where I lose control of his hair. Some boys in our area are beginning to wear crew cuts to bug their parents. Do you think that if I keep my mouth shut there's a chance he'll go in that direction when he decides to rebel? I *love* crew cuts! *Not a chance, right?*

> *There's so much of their lives I can't control now, Lord, even though they're still living with us. Teach me what's important and what isn't, so I'll know when to put my foot down and when to back off.*

Fathers, provoke not your children to anger, lest they be discouraged.

Colossians 3:21

51 Dorm Rooms

I've seen lots of dorm rooms in my lifetime, certainly more than necessary, and they all have one thing in common: If they were used to house convicted felons, the ACLU would shut them down in a week.

Dorm rooms are depressing. They have one high window (50-50 chance it opens), one radiator (75-25 against its working properly), four walls (even money they're painted prison green), and a bare floor (80-20 it's chipped linoleum).

Dorm furniture is army-barracks stark: two sad-looking, not-quite-twin beds, two desks, two small dressers with sticking drawers. This furniture may be either wood or metal, but it will certainly be ugly. Either way, it barely fits into the room.

The room will have one closet for sharing. If it's your son you're taking to college, this presents no problem. If it's your daughter, make sure she gets to the room before her roommate checks in!

This is where your child will live for the next four years. The child who has the biggest bedroom in your house, with two closets filled to the brim, one wall of overflowing cabinets, and room for the old sofa you tried to throw away. Luckily, his favorite storage place has always been under his bed.

It's very hard to leave a child behind in a place like this, even if his roommate's there to keep him company. It's obvious they have to rearrange the furniture to fit in the TV, rented refrigerator, and stereo. They should buy some throw rugs and curtains to brighten the place up a little. Maybe a poster or two, over the desks.

But you've already made his bed and helped him unpack. Too bad no one thought to bring a fan. Your husband's looking pointedly at his watch, thinking of the long drive home. You've given your son the check for opening his bank account. What more can you do?

"Well, I guess we'd better go." *He didn't bring his bedspread. His roommate did.*

"Okay. See you."

"You'll have to introduce yourself to your neighbors." *He probably left his jacket in the closet at home.*

"I will."

"Good-bye. Call us later in the week?" *Where's the pay phone? Does he have quarters?*

"I will. Bye."

Most boys don't cry when you leave them there in that lonely room. All mothers do.

I know he's ready for college, Lord, and I thought I was, too, but does he have to live there? He doesn't know anyone. It must be scary for him; it certainly is for me. Protect him. Help him adjust to his new world. Help me adjust to life without him in my house.

Behold, the hour cometh, yea, is now come, that ye shall be scattered, every man to his own, and shall leave me alone: and yet I am not alone, because the Father is with me.

John 16:32

52 New Worries

Your son's been away at college for a solid month now. You've talked to him briefly and know he's still alive, yet you're walking around with a vague sense of unease hanging over your head. Something's wrong, but you don't know what.

It's new worries, that's all. Your old worries are pretty much irrelevant now, and you haven't named your new worries yet. You have to do that—name them. Then you can look at each of them in turn, laugh off those that are unworthy, and concentrate on the legitimate ones.

Here, let me help. I'll name some of them for you and give you some trial answers, then let you take it from there.

- *Is he eating properly?* No. But one way or another, he is eating. Some things never change. Send vitamins.

- *Does he like his roommate?* No. But they won't come to blows. Send fudge.

- *Is he homesick?* Yes. But he probably won't tell you about it. Write every week.

- *Is he doing well in his classes?* Not as well as he did in high school, but freshmen rarely do. Have faith in him. Send popcorn.

- *Is he safe in that town?* Maybe. College students watch out for one another pretty well. Send brownies to his whole dorm floor.

- *Is he ever coming home again?* As soon as his money's gone and all his jeans are dirty. Send Tide and a tiny check, so it's his choice.

That's most of them, although you may think of more. They're not too bad, are they? Only one problem: You can deal with all these and still not feel right, because what's really bothering you is this one:

- *Now that he's off on is own, does he still love and need me?* Of course he does. You're his mother!

I know he's having the time of his life, Father, and I want that for him, but I miss him. I need a hug!

I will not leave you comfortless: I will come to you.

John 14:18

Home Cooking

How soon they forget!

Send a child off to college and listen to him scream about the cafeteria's food. He's *starving*, he wails on the phone. Send food he can eat in his room.

You go out and spend fifty dollars at the Grand Union for nutritious food that doesn't rot: dry salami, processed cheese, peanut butter, crackers, dried fruit, ready-to-eat pudding. You send up containers of popcorn, boxes of apples, an extra check so he can order pizza on really bad nights.

Kids know how to get to their mothers. From the moment they're born, they know enough to open their mouths and cry hunger. Mother always responds. All over this well-fed nation, mothers are sitting at home nights wondering if their college children are starving to death. They send off packages of vitamins, knowing full well that no college student ever eats a vegetable. They look up the symptoms of scurvy and rickets and order a thirty-dollar box of oranges delivered to the dorm. They sneak wheat germ into the next batch of brownies they ship off. Mothers can be counted on to answer any cries of hunger with enthusiasm, promptness, and ingenuity.

It's best not to dwell on what happens to all that food you send out in love, but most of the dried stuff will come home with him in May. Popcorn is eaten during TV football games; apples and oranges are generally used as ammunition when the snowballs run out. Who knows what happens to all those vitamins, but they do have a very healthy-looking dog living in the dorm.

Schools with awful food services know it and provide a tiny kitchen on each dorm floor, as well as make infinitesimal refrigerators available for rent. Your son's refrigerator will be too full of junk to hold any real food, but he may learn to warm up canned spaghetti and meatballs during the course of four years.

Whole industries spring up in the depressed areas around colleges to feed the starving masses. Chicken, pizza, hamburgers, Chinese food—they can order almost anything delivered to their dorm rooms, for a price.

When he comes home over Thanksgiving, your son will eat from morning to night, uttering quiet sounds of joy as he demolishes the turkey and reaches for the pie. He'll tell you, through his actions and his words, that there's *nothing* as good as your cooking. By the time he leaves for college with a cooler full of whatever's left in your refrigerator, the circles under his eyes will be gone and his face will be filled out again. You've done your job well, and he may just survive until Christmas vacation.

This cycle continues throughout the school year until summer vacation. Then, after two weeks of filling up and out, your son disappears from your dinner table. He either comes home two hours late for dinner or not all. If he should be there on time, he won't be hungry. You can go on cooking him a chop if you want—it makes the dog happy—but he won't want to eat with you until the night you decide *not* to cook for him.

It's frustrating. There he is, right at home, and you can't feed him! Give it up. Soon enough he'll go back to school and call to tell you he's *starving*. Then you can go back to being the best cook in the world.

Father, You've designed all mothers to love feeding their children, to worry about their well-being and care for them. It comes to us naturally and is hard to give up when our children grow old enough to care for themselves. Ease my mind when he's not at my table. Help me to trust in his ability to feed himself. It would also make me feel a lot better if You could arrange for him to develop a sudden craving for leafy green vegetables, but Thy will be done on that one.

She is like the merchants' ships; she bringeth her food from afar.

Proverbs 31:14

54 Clothes

I didn't know clothing was that complex a subject for a teenage boy. After years of being satisfied just to see them fully dressed in the mornings, my standards apparently need to be raised. This didn't occur to me until Jim's girlfriend felt it necessary to take him and his credit card (issued for emergencies while away at college) out to buy him some "decent" clothes.

Now, I'll admit he wasn't a vision of sartorial splendor in his T-shirts and Levi's, but that was what every other nineteen-year-old seemed to be wearing, and he was happy. It took Christmas to get him into real shoes and a pair of slacks. If we went to a resort, he'd manage to find a tie and jacket for dinner. Other than that, it was sneakers and jeans and T-shirts advertising dangerous-looking rock groups.

Okay, I admitted, I might be out of touch. Nineteen was approaching adulthood; maybe his tastes had matured. I said we'd pay the bill when it arrived and waited impatiently for his next visit home.

He came in wearing sneakers and jeans and a T-shirt. The T-shirt was pink. It had an abstract design on the back and the initials OP on the pocket.

"Is that it? What else did you buy?"

"A green OP and a yellow Yukon shirt from Banana Republic. I'm experimenting with colors."

In case you don't have a nineteen-year-old, a Yukon shirt is the top half of a pair of long johns. "Did you buy any new pants?"

"I have black jeans I wear when I get dressed up."

"Levi's?"

"Yeah. But black."

This did not strike me as a revolution in clothing styles, but I wasn't the expert.

"Does your girlfriend like the way you dress now?"

"Yeah. She picked them out."

Okay. Apparently the initials on the pocket were what counted. Or the store he shopped at. Or the colors. Sure looked like the same old Jim to me, though. I was hoping for shoes, slacks, and a real shirt.

His old gang of high school friends arrived in their sneakers, Levi's, and rock-group T-shirts with the sleeves torn out. As they piled out the back door together, I heard one say to Jim, in a voice dripping with sarcasm, "Nice shirt, Jim! Pink!" Yuk, yuk, yuk.

I breathed a sigh of relief. Imagine what they would have said if I'd gotten my wish and he were wearing real shoes and slacks! I'll never get the hang of it; these subtle nuances of dressing are beyond my senile mind. This fall, I'll give him his clothing allowance and let the female of his choice help him pick out his clothes. I don't think there'll be any radical changes I can't handle.

I don't understand their dress code, Lord. I don't much like it, either, but as long as they stay within the bounds of decency, I'll stay out of it. Soon enough he's going to have to wear a suit five days a week. Give me the grace to let him enjoy his freedom while he can.

For if there come unto your assembly a man with a gold ring, in goodly apparel, and there come in also a poor man in vile raiment; And ye have respect to him that weareth the gay clothing, and say unto him, Sit thou here in a good place; and say to the poor, Stand thou there, or sit here under my footstool: Are ye not then partial in yourselves, and are become judges of evil thoughts?

James 2:2–4

55 Maturity

It's 8:00 A.M. on a rainy Sunday morning. As usual, I was wide-awake at 7:00. The coffeepot is burbling away, the cat's been fed, the dog's been let out. Bill's sleeping in, at least until the smell of fresh coffee reaches his brain and he hears the dog bark at the paperboy.

It's quiet. More quiet than normal, it seems, but that may be because I know Bill and I are alone in the house. Our older son's at college. Our daughter is away for the weekend. Our younger son stayed at a friend's last night. Two of them will return later today, but for now, they're all gone.

In about three years, this is what life will be like. I don't know if I'm going to like it. And yet I'm surprised by the peace I feel. I know they're all well. I don't have to worry about waking anyone up on time, and I don't have to cook breakfast unless Bill and I decide we want something to eat. If we want, we can even go out and order ourselves bacon, eggs, and hash browns at the diner.

My daughter's right: We have to start going out more often. We need to invite the neighbors in and to go away by ourselves on weekends. I need to lose twenty pounds, and he needs to start exercising. We need to learn how to talk to each other again as husband and wife, not as Mommy and Daddy. Our lives have revolved around our children for over twenty years; it's time we started learning how to live as individuals.

I don't think this is going to be easy to accomplish. I'm not used to thinking about what *I* want to do instead of how many children I have to feed dinner and who's out of clean clothes. Luckily, I don't have to change overnight. I can work into it slowly over the next three years, while our last child plows through the last half of his teenage years. He'll keep me occupied for a while longer and ease the transition.

The kids will like this process. It's time I got off their backs and set them free. They don't need a clinging mother any more than I need clinging adult children. As long as they don't get too carried away with their freedom, that is! I still want to sit at the kitchen table while my son eats leftover lasagna on a quick visit home from college and listen to him tell me about his life. I want to hear my daughter talk to her father about stocks and bonds and marvel that she's turned into such a smart, charming young woman. I want to watch our youngest mature and grow and see what he'll make of his life.

But I no longer need to know where they are every minute of the day. I'm no longer responsible for keeping their bones intact and their teeth brushed. It's time I started worrying about my own bones and teeth.

I guess it's time I started growing up, too. With a little help, I may turn out to be a credit to my children.

They were tiny babies just days ago, Lord. Now they're young adults, making their own decisions, leading their own lives. Thank You for all the help You've given us over the past years. Be with them, now and forever.

Children's children are the crown of old men; and the glory of children are their fathers.

Proverbs 17:6